BEHIND THE LINES

BEHIND THE LINES

*The Private War
against Soviet Censorship*

DONALD R. SHANOR

St. Martin's Press
New York

Library of Congress Cataloging in Publication Data

Shanor, Donald R.
  Behind the lines.

  1. Mass media—Censorship—Soviet Union. 2. Censorship—Soviet Union. 3. Communication—Soviet Union. 4. Freedom of information—Soviet Union. 5. Soviet Union—Cultural policy. I. Title.
P96.C42S657 1985   302.2'34'0947   84–23797
ISBN 0-312-07265-1

First Edition

10 9 8 7 6 5 4 3 2 1

To Elsie and Katherine

CONTENTS

ACKNOWLEDGMENTS

A book that deals with news, rumor, and opinion must depend on the information and views of many people. A book that deals with the Soviet Union must be very cautious in identifying some of those people. As a result of these conflicting considerations, the list of those whose help I gratefully acknowledge is considerably shorter than it otherwise would be.

My wife Constance and daughters Rebecca and Lisa, for their encouragement, head the list, followed by five colleagues who took the time and trouble to read all or part of the manuscript: Jim Anderson, Dr. Kazimierz Bilanow, W. Phillips Davison, Robert J. Korengold, and Igor Reichlin.

Thanks are also due these organizations: AT&T; Columbia University; ComSat; the Committee for Absorption of Soviet Émigrés, Jersey City; Freedom House; IBM; the Institute of U.S.A. and Canada Studies, Moscow; the Oceanfront YMHA, Brighton Beach; the Osteuropa Institut, Munich; Radio Free Europe/Radio Liberty; the Veterans of World War II Who Emigrated to the U.S. from the U.S.S.R., Brighton Beach; and the Voice of America.

And to these individuals: Ludmilla Alexeyeva, Pauline Beilus, Edward Brown, James F. Brown, Bridie Cooke, Nick and Ruth Daniloff, Wade Doares, Dusko Doder, Ira Fuchs, Barbara Futterman, Mark Hopkins, Ben Lederman, Pavel Litvinov, Gerald Long, Natalia Lusin, Gerard Mansell, Bryan May, Barbara Moldauer, Alexander Motyl, Bill Mullane, Andrew Nemethy, Sam and Annette Rachlin, Robert Rooney, David Saltman, Eleanor Singer,

Pat Singer, Ned Temko, Ludmilla Thorne, and Richard Troiano. Barbara Anderson, my editor, deserves special mention for long-distance guidance.

None of the individuals or institutions that helped in the preparation of the book can be held responsible for its imperfections, content, or findings, which remain my sole responsibility.

—Donald R. Shanor
June 1984
Chappaquiddick Island, Massachusetts

BEHIND THE LINES

• 1 •

The University of the Millions

The control of information is one of the three basic instruments of rule in the Soviet system, the second being the Party's monopoly on decision-making in politics, the economy, and culture; and the third being the police. Information control is the weakest of the three. The state monopoly has been broken by unofficial news networks linking ordinary citizens as well as dissidents. Information technology—computers and satellites—is outpacing the state's restraints.

Foreign broadcasts play such an important part in informing people in the Soviet Union that some Soviet citizens call them the "University of the Millions." The name is a takeoff on a televised program of political education that is broadcast on one of the government channels at six P.M., when viewers might be expected to want something a little lighter.

This book is about these unofficial networks and the officially controlled media system that makes them necessary. It examines the impact on Soviet society and public opinion of new and independent sources of news and trustworthy information after decades of one-sided propaganda. At issue is more than the internal Soviet problem of managing news in a closed society. A better-informed Soviet public can play an important role in creating a better international climate.

A Soviet citizen who spends the day in a government office or factory surrounded by production pledges and peace posters, who attends a noontime lecture on current events delivered by a Party agitator, who takes a bus ride home past banners explaining the benefits of Communism and glances through newspapers devoted to the same task, is well aware of the importance of controlled information on daily existence.

But the controls falter when he or she closes the apartment door and enters the unorganized realm of private life. With the exception of the evening news, television fare is often not very appealing; if the schedule shows only political education or war films, he or she is likely to turn them off and look for other kinds of information. These alternate channels can't be reached through the television set—at least, not yet—but they are only a visit or a telephone call away, when friend talks to friend to relate news of the workplace, hear gossip from the canteen, repeat what is being broadcast on the BBC or the Voice of America, or tell what satirical poems or songs have recently been privately taped.

Technology already speeds the reception and exchange of information along this network. Radios have become cheaper, portable, and more powerful. Direct telephone dialing within the Soviet Union makes it easier to contact friends and relatives in other cities and harder for the police to eavesdrop. Technological development will expand the channels of information in the very near future. Television programs could be beamed from satellites directly into Soviet homes, either deliberately, as with a video Voice of America, or as the accidental by-product of the satellite transmissions used in Western European broadcasting.

That would be bad news for the producers of Soviet television programs like the real "University of the Millions," which does have millions of viewers, in part because it is tied in with a home study program for degree credit and job advancement, in part because there is little else to watch.

What would happen if a click of the channel selector could produce Alexander Solzhenitsyn, sitting in the study of his Vermont home surrounded by books Soviet citizens can't read, and, like a Russian Alistair Cooke, introducing the next episode of the "Gulag Archipelago"? ("In our last episode, you'll recall, we were describing the 'ships of the Archipelago,' the prison trains with compartments designed for six men and packed with as many as thirty-five for journeys as long as three weeks.") Or if another click could bring the BBC's Russian-language news, with film on the war in Afghanistan and details about disputes among the Kremlin leaders? A further channel could be carrying exiled director Yuri Lyubimov's staging of *The Master and Margarita*, the satire on Soviet bureaucracy that was long banned by that bureaucracy; another, a popular Swedish rock group, also banned.

The possibilities are endless; the technology is readily available. Viewers who live on the Baltic coast of the Soviet Union or close to its western borders are already watching the broadcasts of foreign television stations. With direct transmissions from satellites, everyone in the nation could have a picture of showroom clarity, with the sound in Russian or other Soviet languages.

Technologically possible, politically impossible. The Soviet regime's efforts to maintain its information monopoly, what Milovan Djilas[1] has called "the exclusive right to determine what the individual may feel and think," are immense. If there is to be an information revolution in the Soviet Union, it will not take place with the approval of the Party.

Direct Broadcast by Satellite, DBS, would constitute such a threat that the Soviet leadership probably would order the transmitting satellites shot down. That, at least, is the opinion both of Western broadcast specialists who have studied the possibility and of Soviet officials interviewed for this book.

But as the information revolution sweeps through almost every other country in the world, as television sets shrink to wristwatch size, telephones lose their cords, radios get smaller and stronger, computers talk to their operators and each other, and the electronic signals that link all these devices crisscross in space, 22,300 miles above national borders, it becomes clear that there are already too many targets for the Soviet leaders to shoot down. The KGB started to lose the information battle in the era of Nikita Khrushchev, when the jamming of foreign broadcasts was first suspended. When Soviet engineers, some years after the West, introduced direct telephone dialing between cities, it was another defeat for the eavesdroppers. Personal computers, bought off the shelf in Japan or the West, are beginning to show up in Soviet

---

1. In an interview with George Urban for Urban's book *Stalinism* (New York: St. Martin's Press, 1982).

home offices, and every one is a potential printing press as well as a link to other computers. Satellites launched to improve Western Europe's television transmission and to bring in American programming are beaming down signal "footprints" that can be picked up across the Soviet border. The Soviet hobbyists' magazine *Radio* has already printed instructions on how to make your own audio tape recorder; can video recorder plans be far behind? Until they arrive, hundreds if not thousands of video recorders are being privately imported, and it is doubtful that many of them are used for taping a missed segment of "University of the Millions." The favorite video cassettes include forbidden American movies, smuggled-in Scandinavian sex films, and television programs taped from Finnish broadcasts that reach the Soviet side of the Baltic.

The KGB can go around pulling all these plugs, knocking down dish antennae that are pointed at Europe's satellites, erasing tapes and tapping telephone lines. But in the process it will be interfering with the communication links the regime considers legitimate: the computers used by scientists and economists, the broadcasts of the domestic stations, even the entertainment of Party officials able to afford to buy a video tape recorder for about the same price as that of a new car. There are plenty of examples in Soviet history of ideology triumphing over practicality; farm production could probably be doubled, for instance, if peasants were allowed to increase the size of their private plots. But in the information field, the regime already has yielded considerable ground, and seems ill-equipped to understand the changes in speed and style of communication taking place internationally. While Soviet scientists try to catch up with their Western and Japanese counterparts, often with brilliant innovations in satellite transmission technology or computer usage, another vast arm of the government is still employed in censoring every tiny bit of information made public in more than nine copies, including the text on matchbook covers.

In its attempt to hold back the information revolution, the Party has drawn a line that clearly shows what is not permissible. But because it wants to take advantage of advances in communications for its own needs, it has also had to designate a rather large area of activities that will be tolerated. The deliberate transmission of DBS television programs into the Soviet Union cannot be permitted, and the Soviet representatives at international conferences have worked hard to have that viewpoint accepted by the world. Other Soviet diplomats have been trying to influence the size and shape of European satellite footprints, to prevent spillover into their territory, and to persuade European broadcasters to transmit only scrambled signals that cannot be picked up by a video hobbyist with a homemade antenna.

But the line keeps bending. The radios made in the state electronics factories are built without the capacity to pick up any foreign shortwave broadcast. But every high school tinkerer knows how to convert them. Those who want to pay a stiff price for a foreign portable radio that will pull in all kinds of broadcasts and tape-record them besides can find them easily—in the state-run secondhand stores. The regime fights DBS at the United Nations but plugs its ships and land stations into the Western-developed INMARSAT navigation and information system. It starts, and then stops, domestic production of video tape recorders, and then permits *Literaturnaya Gazeta* to reverse the official position on the social ill effects of video: "Video equipment opens up fantastic opportunities. . . . The social role which the video cassette is to play in our lives is huge, comparable with the emergence of cinema and television."

In the meantime, officialdom manages to pretend that the old information monopoly is intact. When Leonid Brezhnev died, the news was kept from the people and the world for twenty-five hours. Yuri Andropov was dead almost twenty-four hours before the news was announced. During both of these periods, the shortwaves crackled with Western speculation, filed by correspondents in Moscow. When the official announcements did come, it was almost an anticlimax.

The monopoly worked well, however, in keeping Andropov's illness secret. Dr. Ira Greifer, medical director of the National Kidney Foundation, believes that Andropov was no longer ambulatory after August 1983, six months before his death, and might even have had a leg amputated.[2] As late as December a

---

2. As stated in a letter to the author.

senior Kremlin spokesman, Leonid Zamyatin, continued to insist that the Soviet president and party chief's illness was only a cold. All through the autumn, Andropov was depicted as writing speeches and statements, sending letters abroad, and presenting intricate plans to the Supreme Soviet for economic reform. "It is quite obvious that he was not physically or medically alert to be able to really run the government," Dr. Greifer said. "The autopsy, as stated by the Russian government, described far advanced wasting of his internal organs, again giving strong evidence that he was sick and debilitated for a long time before his recognized death."

The secrecy about Andropov's illness had a political rationale. At a time of rivalry and uncertainty in the top ranks of the Party, it would not have been to Moscow's advantage to let the world know of Andropov's incapacity. Such a course is possible only in countries where the press can be silenced and no official dares to leak information or speculate on such high-level matters. But there seemed to be no justification for the other secret of Andropov's brief term of office, the existence of his wife. When a middle-aged woman appeared at his funeral, the same officials who had described Andropov as a widower to Western correspondents identified her as Mrs. Tatyana Andropov, who had secretly reigned as Soviet First Lady for fifteen months. Reporters' efforts to learn if she was a first or second wife, mother or stepmother of the President's two grown children, were shrugged off.

When a Soviet pilot shot down the Korean Airlines passenger jet over Sakhalin island, with the loss of 269 lives, Pravda first maintained that an unidentified aircraft had intruded into Soviet air space but had left it unharmed. Two days later, reacting to Western accounts of the incident and worldwide condemnation, TASS repeated this version, but then expressed regret for the loss of life, which it blamed on the Americans who had sent the plane on a spy mission. It took a further four days for the government to acknowledge that a fighter pilot of the Air Defense Force had "fulfilled the command station's order to stop the flight."

All these mysteries and contradictions would be puzzling to Soviet readers and listeners, were it not for the existence of their own independent system of information. Anyone with a shortwave radio set knew what had happened to the Korean airliner hours after it disappeared, not days. Anyone who might have missed details of the incident because of jamming or not being able to tune in would have been filled in by friends along the network. And those who want to hear the whole sequence of events in the future can have easy access to one of the many thousands of tapes made during the crisis period.

An event of international significance like a change of leaders in the Kremlin or an attack on a civilian plane serves to throw light on the alternate sources of information available to Soviet citizens. Western correspondents talk to the men and women on the street and learn that they are far better informed about these situations than they could be expected to be if their information were confined to that issued by the state. During the Korean airliner incident, John F. Burns wrote in *The New York Times* from Moscow that a surprising number of people had learned the full story by listening to the Russian-language broadcasts of the BBC, VOA, and the West German station Deutsche Welle. Although the broadcasts were heavily jammed, he said, one man told him that "if you want to listen and keep searching the dial long enough, you'll get a signal." As a result, Burns wrote, the words used by such people to describe the fate of the airliner's passengers were little different from those heard in the West.

But what happens in the case of news events of less importance? How does word get around on the trends, ideas, fads, fashions, and even ideologies that are ignored by the Soviet media? To explore the day-to-day operation of the Soviet Union's underground telegraph, the author conducted interviews in the Soviet Union and in the Soviet exile communities of the United States and Western Europe. More than 150 people were interviewed, about half in the Soviet Union, during three visits totaling more than two months, and half in the West. In addition, more than 600 questionnaires were sent to Soviet émigrés in the United States and about seventy returned.

The rate of return is unusually low by American standards, but not by Soviet or Soviet exile ones. In Brighton Beach, the section of Brooklyn heavily populated with Soviet émigrés, the chamber of commerce once issued a special invitation to the fifty émigré owners of businesses to join the 150 Americans already in the group. An informal meeting was arranged; the émigrés were to be honored for their contribution to reinvigorating what had been a decaying part of the city. Only one showed up.

Business people and social workers who know the émigré community say it takes years for them to lose their suspicion of authority. They simply refuse to give their names or cooperate with anything appearing to be official, such as a chamber of commerce. The appearance of an interviewer with a clipboard full of questionnaires was usually greeted with considerable reserve. Only when anonymity was promised did some of the former Soviet citizens agree to cooperate. Many said they were worried about causing trouble for relatives still in the Soviet Union. Others showed the skills of evasion and obfuscation learned in decades of coping with the Soviet system. For these reasons (and the more compelling needs of those interviewed in the USSR) the pages that follow have fewer names and identifications attached to quotations and opinions than the author would like.

With a range of interviews that included the most loyal and enthusiastic Party officials as well as the most pessimistic and conspiracy-obsessed dissidents, there is also a considerable range of what might be considered facts or truth. How can a way be charted between the extremes? Taking the middle is not necessarily the best method, because sometimes the fringes turn out to be right. The author, as a journalist, used the tried and often true methods of the journalist: registering an assertion as probably true when enough different sources and viewpoints converged to make it seem plausible. In this way, claims that the two extremes would make—that the Soviet Union is a fully participatory society, from the one fringe, or that it is a KGB state, run by the secret police at every level from Politburo to workplace, from the other—could be sorted out and evaluated.

The careful practices of survey research, as used in the United States and other Western countries, are clearly left behind in this methodology. To get a random sampling of the population of the Soviet Union to respond to a questionnaire or an interview by a Westerner would be impossible under the social conditions likely to prevail there for some time. Nor is the situation much better among the Soviet émigrés in the United States. The 30,000 émigrés in and around Brighton Beach are not representative of the Soviet population, nor are the 60,000 to 70,000 in New York, nor the nearly 200,000 in the United States.

Indeed, it could be argued, there are two factors that make their experience and opinions so much at variance with those of the citizens who stayed in the Soviet Union that they should be viewed with great reserve. The first is emigration. They chose to leave the country, and could be expected to have little positive to say about it, and a great deal that is negative. At the same time, they could be expected to want to ingratiate themselves with the Americans in their new home—the flattery factor that researchers try to allow for when asking questions of refugees and immigrants.

The second obstacle is the fact that the vast majority of Soviet émigrés in the United States are Jews, which adds the status of disadvantaged minority to that of someone who has rejected the Soviet system.

There is no question that it would have been better to have done all the research for this book in the Soviet Union. That this was not the case is not entirely the author's fault. He was twice nominated by the U.S. Fulbright Commission for a senior lectureship at the Faculty of Journalism of Moscow State University, under an informal agreement between the Graduate School of Journalism of Columbia University and the Moscow school. Although two scholars from Moscow had already been granted a year at Columbia to conduct their research, the Soviet faculty twice refused, at nearly the last minute, to honor its part of the agreement.

Dividing the research and interviewing between the Soviet Union and the American exile communities did have its advantages. A claim made in Moscow or Leningrad by an editor, official, or man or woman on the street could be checked against the views of a counterpart in Brighton Beach or Forest Hills. The accounts of the émigrés could be tested on a subsequent Soviet visit with those still in the country.

But is it possible to trust the views of émigrés at all? Their bias, their resentment against the regime that they opposed in their old homes, as well as their discontent with their new lives, are often cited as good reasons to avoid them as information sources. There are two answers to this question. One is to consider the alternatives: information from official Soviet sources, supported by official Soviet figures, in a nation where the size of the harvest, when it is a bad one, is a state secret. The other is that if refugee sources are discounted, then much of what we think we know about closed societies around the world should also be discounted, including landmark studies like the Harvard Project on the Soviet Social System, based on refugee interviews after World War II, as well as the Rand Corporation's work on the Hungarian revolution and the Polish and Soviet systems of media and censorship.[3]

The best testimonial to the reliability of careful use of refugee sources, however, comes from the periodic revelations of the leaders or intellectuals of the closed societies themselves. Khrushchev's 1956 secret speech on Stalin's crimes corroborated everything the exiles had been saying, and indeed showed that some of them had been guilty of understatement. The uncensored Czech and Slovak press of 1968, and the Polish press of the Solidarity years, carried daily revelations by Communist officials that confirmed the information provided Western analysts by refugees about the state of the economy and society.

But the question of the reliability of the information provided by many of those whose views are used in this book must still be addressed. Are Soviet Jews so different from other Soviet citizens as to make their experiences invalid? It was a question that those being interviewed often answered without being asked.

One kind of answer stressed the differences. It would sometimes be expressed as an aside during an interview: "Write letters to the editor? No, none of our family ever did. It seemed that it might draw attention to us, and that we didn't want. We're Jews, after all."

In other cases, the issue of Jewish emigration came up. Some

---

3. The Harvard Project's books include *How the Soviet System Works*, by Bauer, Inkeles, and Kluckhohn (Cambridge: Harvard University Press, 1956), as well as specialized studies like Mark Field's *Doctor and Patient in Soviet Russia*. Rand studies include Paul Kecskemeti's *The Unexpected Revolution*, *The Media and Intra-Elite Communication in Poland*, by Jane Leftwich Curry and A. Ross Johnson, and *The Media and Intra-Elite Communication in the USSR*, by Dzirkals, Gustafson, and Johnson.

respondents said they had worried about too much listening to foreign broadcasts or passing on information. They did not want to get into trouble with the authorities and hurt their chances of leaving the country. But others appeared to have extra-sensitive antennae for news from the private information networks, since it could have a bearing on their hopes for leaving.

The other kind of answer stressed the similarities. "We were the super Soviet citizens, because we are Jewish. Until détente, at the start of the seventies, no one had ever thought there would be any hope of being able to leave the Soviet Union. It was stay and make the best of it. After the experiences of the Stalin years, when anti-Semitism was always just beneath the surface, if not worse, we knew we had to become model citizens and get ahead."

A final point to consider is the effect on recollections of life in the Soviet Union caused by later experiences. Are émigrés who can choose among the three New York daily newspapers, cable and network television news, competing Russian-language papers, all-news radio programs, and dozens of magazines able to recall what it was like to live in an information-hungry society? "I didn't even know what public opinion was until I came here," a student said in an interview. But further questioning showed that he was able to identify some aspects of the public opinion process from his earlier experience. After all, Gallup and Harris don't expect those who are randomly sampled to know what that means.

There are many perils in assessing the state of information and opinion in a society that spends a considerable effort in promoting a picture of itself that by any honest measurement is at variance with the facts. The only real assurance the author can provide is that the research was conducted and the conclusions drawn as fairly and objectively as he knows how, knowing also that those concepts are rejected energetically—at least for public consumption—by the Soviet media establishment members he interviewed.

· 2 ·

The Grand Illusion

Every night at nine P.M., most of the 100 million Soviet television sets are tuned to the same program: *"Vremya,"* or *"Time,"* the evening news. *"Vremya"*'s content, format, and point of view are so vastly different from those of Western television programs that it is difficult to make a comparison on the same terms. Both have field correspondents, anchors, editors, and camera crews, and both have a regular spot on the evening viewing schedules, adjusted for differences in time zones. Here the resemblance stops. The studio backdrop of the red brick Kremlin walls and towers on *"Vremya"* is more than just a setting for some of the main events of the day, as the White House or Houses of Parliament are. The Kremlin not only makes news but controls it, by determining what may and may not be broadcast as well as what must be.

"Vremya" is carried on every channel (most cities have three or four; Moscow has five). A Soviet joke says that everyone's television set has an additional channel on which a uniformed KGB official appears to tell you to turn back to the others and watch *"Vremya."* Soviet viewers wouldn't need this device. They have no choice but the off button, unless they belong to the small percentage of the population that lives close enough to other countries to eavesdrop on foreign television. With information such a scarce commodity in Soviet society, the opportunity to hear news, any news, even that coming out of the Kremlin pipeline, keeps most of the sets on. There are no Nielsen ratings published in the USSR, but interviews of Soviet citizens and the experience of

Westerners in the Soviet Union show that *"Vremya"* is widely watched.

With no competing network, and with news supervised, if not written, by the propaganda experts of the Central Committee, *"Vremya"* is a direct line from government to citizen. Moreover, because of a production program that pushed Soviet television-set ownership from 18 million in the mid-1960s to 100 million at the beginning of the 1980s (compared to 90 million and 170 million for the United States) it probably has the largest regular audience of any news program in the world.

China, which usually excels in comparisons involving large numbers of people, has many more potential viewers and an information system just as tightly knit, but has produced only about fifteen million television sets.

The United States' larger news audiences are split among three commercial networks and a public one as well as independent stations' news programs, cable news, and the distractions of game shows and rerun comedies. The White House can command an audience the size of *"Vremya"*'s from time to time, for presidential speeches or press conferences. But it must count on the president's words being interpreted or contradicted by independent journalists equally and sometimes more credible to the viewers than the president himself.

Moscow need not worry about this possibility. *"Vremya"*'s journalists work for the government, and only in rare cases have departed even slightly from the directives of the Central Committee Propaganda Department and Glavlit, the government's Main Administration for Safeguarding State Secrets in the Press.

"Vremya," in fact, is a perfect example of the New World Information Order, the system that encourages governments to control the news their citizens receive. The first step is to make sure that most people have access to newspapers, radios, and television sets, and in this, the Soviet Union rates high in UNESCO statistics. The second is to exclude any competing voices, so that only a single, uncomplicated version of events and a single, unassailable interpretation of issues can exist. The result should be the efficient and unfettered transmission of information of the kind the

government wants its citizens to have and deems that the citizens need (and only that kind).

In the Soviet Union, what results instead is a grand illusion: made-up news, counterfeit views, and a picture of reality that very few of the men, women, and children in front of the television sets can accept or recognize, unless it concerns situations so far from their daily lives in subject or distance that they have no independent means of judging the truth. Instead of informing, *"Vremya"* produces mostly propaganda. Instead of communicating, it campaigns. Instead of focusing on the problems of the nation and telling its millions of viewers how their government is coping with them, it hides them, ignores them, or lies about them. What is true of the evening news on television is, of course, true of every other medium of communication, from films to newspapers.

If American television news were written by journalists employed by the White House press office, and if the programs were produced by advertising agencies from Madison Avenue, under an arrangement in which competing journalists could be arrested, the effect would be about the same. A costly war on the nation's borders could be all but ignored; disastrous harvests could be depicted as triumphs; economic stagnation could be labeled unprecedented progress.

Soviet citizens do learn about the fighting in Afghanistan and the harvest and other economic failures, but they do so despite, not because of, the official coverage. They do not dismiss the official versions of events out of hand, however. In an information-hungry society, they scan the government media for any scraps of news they might contain. Sometimes the information is there because someone—in the ministry originating the report, the Party department checking it, or the newsroom preparing it for the public—has slipped. Less often, an item could be interesting because a journalist was willing to take risks and had the support of his or her editors. Both slips and risk-taking occur far less frequently in the Soviet Union than in other nations with a controlled press, including the Communist countries of Eastern Europe.

Soviet officials are not at all uncomfortable with the idea of rigid controls on information. At UNESCO, they join with the authoritarian Third World nations in trying to impose such controls on the international flow of information, and at home, they defend the notion that government and press are partners, never adversaries. Lenin's 1902 description of the newspaper as "not only collective propagandist and collective agitator, but also collective organizer" is not something they brush aside as perhaps suitable for a revolutionary group seeking power but no longer acceptable for a modern society that transmits its news by satellite. Lenin's words are brought up on the frequent press anniversaries and are stressed as guides to action for today's journalists: propagandists, agitators, and organizers.

Information is the ingredient absent from Lenin's prescription, and for the readers of *Pravda*, the newspaper he helped found, and the other eight thousand dailies and weeklies, this poses problems. To extract information, Soviet readers know they must skim through what they call the ceremonial part of articles that interest them and concentrate on the "shortcomings and solutions" section at the end. They must wait for ten minutes or so of harvest news at the start of *"Vremya"*'s late-summer programs to find out what is going on in the world, and in other seasons sit through the long stories about factories and mines that have overfulfilled their plans.

At harvest time, the combines roll across the sunny fields of the Ukraine and Kazakhstan on every evening of *"Vremya."* There may be fighting in the Middle East or a breakthrough in a Geneva conference, but the real news can wait. As in the United States, the advertising people have to have their allotment of time, and in the Soviet Union, the only advertiser is the government. The harvest or factory commercials, at least, come at the start of the news and do not interrupt it.

The combines make interesting patterns in the grain fields of the various Soviet agricultural regions as news crews film them from the side, the front, above. Then come shots of collective farm chairmen being given medals for raising more grain than others; shots of little girls giving bouquets to collective farm workers, sunburned male tractor and combine drivers and sunburned women, usually with hand tools. Television's performance is repeated in the morning papers, with combine and collective farmer pictures spread across the top of front pages.

The commentaries could be mistaken for military communiqués, so frequently do they refer to victories and triumphs over adverse conditions, calling in reserves, and organizing logistics. As with news released by the military, they need have no connection with the truth. *"Vremya"*'s daily accounts of victorious campaigns on the grain front are produced for the public without the slightest regard for the actual situation in agriculture. The succession of poor harvests of the final Brezhnev years were getting television coverage worthy of the battle for Berlin while they were in progress. Western journalists in Moscow could learn from Soviet sources and diplomats that the harvests were disasters instead of triumphs, and pass that on to their readers. Those Soviet citizens who had not learned this by reading between the lines were soon to learn it from standing in lines.

If the Soviet media err on the side of positive news at home, they balance this by stressing negative developments abroad. There is always a great deal of conflict in the news, but it all takes place in Southern Africa, Northern Ireland, or Central America, far from the borders of supposedly conflict-free Russia. Routine changes of government in Belgium or Costa Rica are treated as the sensations they would be if they took place in Moscow. The United States is a land of unemployment, racism, and militarism, and is responsible for these ills in almost every other country that gets mentioned. The reports on these themes seldom change to fit changing conditions: unemployment in America is attacked during times of prosperity as well as times of recession. When the United States withdrew from Vietnam, it was immediately accused of planning even worse wars. A new Radio Moscow correspondent in the United States reported that his only out-of-town assignment in his first six months had been to cover a Ku Klux Klan rally in Buffalo, an event that rated a paragraph in most American papers.

The nation without conflicts to cover fills the space in its press with accounts of achievements. They are best brought out on the occasion of an anniversary, another of the cyclical phenomena that, along with the harvest and production-plan fulfillment, make the Soviet calendar so crowded and the pages of Soviet newspapers so predictable. It is easy to plan for coverage of anniversaries, as it is for the World Series, because journalists and editors know the dates well in advance. Unlike the World Series, the outcome is also known.

An example is the anniversary of the formation of the Soviet Railway Workers' Union. The specialized publications of the union take the lead in coverage, followed by *Trud*, the trade unions newspaper, with accounts of meetings held and medals bestowed. Editorials hail the importance of the state railway system and its workers. The general press and television pick up the story and publish graphs showing the growth of the system, with many references to the campaign to build the Baikal–Amur line in Siberia. Even the entertainment program at Gorky Park is synchronized. Choruses of railway workers sing for the Sunday crowds, who then go home and find more railway anniversary news on *"Vremya."*

They may have jammed into dirty and antiquated suburban railway cars to get home from the park, stood in long lines to get tickets, put up with overbearing conductors and sloppy safety procedures. None of this has any place in news coverage of the railways—unless the situation gets so bad that one branch of the government uses the media to discipline another, subordinate, branch. Soviet journalists contend that they do as much investigative reporting as their Western counterparts in finding and fixing blame for the many shortcomings of the system. The difference is that they do not act on their own, or as a team with their editors. Only if someone high enough in the appropriate ministry or department of the Central Committee decides that Moscow's suburban train system should run a little more efficiently do the stories about two-hour waits without explanation begin to appear.

As for railway disasters, they do not fit at all in a policy of extolling the achievements of socialism. The practice of ignoring these and other accidents, or of printing a paragraph without casualty details on an inside page, is gradually being replaced by slightly fuller coverage that always contains a lesson. Those responsible are promised punishment; an investigation is already underway; conclusions will be drawn.

The media as teacher. It would be wrong to dismiss the anniversaries, the achievement coverage, as chamber of commerce style back-patting. There is that element, but there are also recurrent themes in the Soviet press that show how highly the good example, whether of an individual or an entire industry, is valued as a means of showing the way to others.

One main message is the need for everyone to work harder and more efficiently so that all can share in a better life. The flowers, the medals, the anniversary banners draped on locomotives, and the women in factory coveralls who get their picture on the front page of *Pravda* all serve this end. If the examples of productivity to be found close at hand do not measure up to these standards, if the workers in one's own factory are noted more for their absentee rate than their triumphs over the plan, there is still a lesson to be drawn. It is that Soviet workers are already far better off than the insecure working people of the West, haunted by unemployment and bread lines.

Another theme is that this better life, after all the decades of struggle, is again threatened, not from the inefficiency of the domestic economy, but by these same outsiders, and others. No propaganda is needed to make Russians dislike Germans, although considerable amounts of it are nevertheless applied. The Americans are the main targets, however, with the Chinese a strong second. Films, articles, short stories, television documentaries by the thousands recall the horror of World War II and warn that the same kinds of forces are ready to strike again. To prevent this, the nation's military men, whether in the Kremlin or on the borders, must be supported, by the sacrifice of consumer goods and money and by waging a peace campaign aimed only at the other side's nuclear weapons and foreign bases.

A third theme is never openly stated. It is a kind of striving for legitimacy, a curious phenomenon for a regime that has at its disposal more arms than any other and a population unlikely to consider any act of opposition more serious than grumbling. One way of looking at the banners of self-praise that adorn Soviet buildings and the anniversary fever is as part of the perpetual campaign to provide new goals and incentives. Another is to view them as signs of insecurity and of the need to be reminded that another year, or decade, or quarter-century has been added to the slowly accumulating store of legitimacy.

Soviet officials and journalists accept the existence of the first two themes and dispute the third. As to the use of the media to mobilize society behind these or any other campaigns, they offer no apologies at all. They look on their roles much as writers and editors for company publications do: if it is good for the company, give it your best. Find those Siberian fishermen with interesting hobbies. Write about the international attention focused on a doctor in the Crimea with new ideas about heart disease. Listen to the stories of the old lady in a Leningrad apartment who once saw Lenin. Soviet journalists who have emigrated say they felt their talents were being put to good use when they carried out assignments like these, and some found it possible to tuck in little elements of mild social criticism in the process.

But the real criticism never gets written, unless there is a clear signal from above. When that happens, the press is a willing ally. The same tiny apartments that are described as cozy in the feature stories become not worthy of families under socialism if a housing scandal is being investigated. The Siberian fishermen are no longer considered colorful if their managers are found to have been skimming off profits. Then, suddenly, these campaigns stop, and it is back to features carefully crafted to push the product—in the case of American company publications, goodwill; in the case of the Soviet, the system.

"The Soviet TASS does *not* claim impartiality in news work," a textbook from the International Organization of Journalists in Prague says. "The concept of 'absolute objectivity' and 'perfect impartiality' is false and unrealistic."

These are clearly the views of Nikolai Tesyadin, a large man with a shaggy shock of gray hair who presides over *Soviet Siberia*, the daily that covers an area larger than Western Europe, from its headquarters in Novosibirsk. Siberia, Russia's East, likes to compare itself to America's West, and the editors of the paper are full of talk of expansion and development, risk-taking, the frontier spirit. Tesyadin was pleased to report during our interview that the order had just come from Moscow to increase circulation by 35,000 copies a day, a 25-percent jump. That meant that readers in Novosibirsk, a city sometimes called the Soviet Chicago, and the nearby research institutes at Akademgorodok, wanted more local news, and that the distant Central Committee propaganda specialists in Moscow had decided that increasing the newsprint supply was justified. (There was enough wood pulp in the forests stretching out from *Soviet Siberia's* plant on the edge of the city to supply every reader in the Soviet Union, but cutting and processing it is another matter.)

What were the local issues that readers found so interesting? Dogs, the editors said. People let their dogs run loose in Novosibirsk. They get in the garbage. Nothing else? Having experienced the buses packed so far beyond their capacity that even in winter riders' legs and shoulders protruded from the doors, I suspected that transit could be a problem. An icy hotel room with plumbing only partly functioning and a refrigerator that didn't function at all suggested to me that if these were the standards in the city's international hotel, those in ordinary blocks of flats might be lower. "It's dogs that we print the most letters to the editor about," Tesyadin said.

The frontier spirit at *Soviet Siberia* stopped short of any independent reporting, but editors conceded that if the city soviet saw fit to draw attention to shortcomings in public transport or housing, the paper would join in with enthusiasm. They offered no apologies for having to get Moscow's permission to sell more papers, only satisfaction that it had been granted.

In any case, Tesyadin stressed, Soviet journalists are not supposed to take adversarial positions; they are all on the same team with the government. In a place like Siberia, which is still developing and expanding, it is all the more important that concepts like impartiality and objectivity be viewed in context. Could a newspaper able to be independently critical save the developers and expanders from some of their mistakes? The editors said they were satisfied that the present system provided plenty of avenues for such criticism.

They were also satisfied, they said, with the arrangement that put Tesyadin at the head of the local journalists' union as well as

in charge of the paper. Discussions sometimes arose about assignments and hours, but the editor–union chairman never had any
trouble resolving them.

In the newsprint allocation, the timidity in taking on local issues, and the co-opting of the union, *Soviet Siberia* was con-
forming to the systems set up by the Party to discourage
independence, whether of newspapers from the government or
of staff members from editors. To have a single person wearing
the hats of chief editor and union chief is a tradition for national
as well as regional papers. *Pravda's* chief editor usually is the national head of the journalists' union. The Central Committee's
propaganda department decides when a new newspaper will be
introduced or when circulation figures will be changed for those
already publishing. Other Party units cooperate by making sure
that the papers are sold. Party members have an obligation to buy
a certain number of papers and journals, and must subscribe to
some of the heavy theoretical ones if they want also to have
lighter reading. Special stress is placed on subscriptions to the
Party daily, *Pravda*, and the theoretical journal, *Kommunist*. This
keeps circulation in the multiple millions, but is, of course, no
guarantee of readership. "*Pravda* was the cheapest way for me to
fulfill my Party obligation," a scientist now in the West said. "But
you'd see a pile of unread ones in my library. If I read anything in
addition to my journals, it was the local Leningrad paper, but I
got no credit in the Party for buying it."

In an economy dominated by the plan, production of goods is
often confused with consumption. This is why there are both
shortages and backlogs of unsold-because-shoddy merchandise in
the Soviet Union. As with manufactured goods, so with printed
ones. In announcing that more copies of Lenin's works had been
printed than those of any other author, the Soviet press said that
this means Lenin has had 600 million *readers*. It seems certain that
at least a part of the run of *What Is to Be Done?* in the Buryat or
Malay languages is resting in some warehouse. In any case, Soviet authors occupy two of the top five places in UNESCO's count
of books printed but not necessarily read. Leonid Brezhnev is
fifth; between him and Lenin are some Western writers whose

works are published more on the basis of demand: Agatha Christie, Jules Verne, and Walt Disney.

Pravda no longer dominates the national press in circulation; that honor has gone to *Trud*, perhaps because there are many more members of the trade unions (almost everyone with a job) than there are of the Party. But there has been no diminution of *Pravda*'s flagship role on matters of what is newsworthy and what course editorial opinion should take. With *Kommunist* and the official news agency TASS, *Pravda* is the authoritative voice of the Communist Party of the Soviet Union, ranked above every other publication or news service, empowered to correct their mistakes and set their line as well as to reject any attempt, however unlikely, on their part to correct *Pravda*'s mistakes or set its line. *Pravda* also dictates the general line and some of the content of the Party dailies of Eastern Europe, although the days when the front pages in every loyal country in the bloc looked alike are gone.

Pravda's editors and even its reporters are deferred to by all but the highest-level officials, at home and abroad, at least in countries where *Pravda* counts. At a reception for dozens of foreign correspondents from East and West in East Berlin, polite but firm waiters held back the representatives of papers like the *Los Angeles Times* and *Neue Zürcher Zeitung* until the *Pravda* man could arrive and have first crack at the buffet table. When he strode into the room, the reception line of high East German officials parted and re-formed into a V to steer him to the smoked salmon and caviar. Later, under the glow of the East Germans' vodka, the *Pravda* man, who had first seen Germany from a Red Army tank, let his Western colleagues in on his private thoughts about the leaders and citizens of the host country, making it plain that he held them in somewhat less than high regard.

Both that correspondent and the editors of *Soviet Siberia* are products of the *nomenklatura* system, the Party's method of controlling all important jobs in the media as well as every other government office. Writing and reporting skills are only incidental requisites in Soviet journalism. *Nomenklatura*-level editors and correspondents often come from other Party or government jobs having nothing to do with journalism. A good record of Party work, career ambitions tempered by caution, and connections in the Party hierarchy, whether at local or higher levels, are what count.

The last two chief editors of *Pravda* have backgrounds that might seem to qualify them to run a government ministry or institute but not a newspaper. Viktor Afanasev held professorships in philosophy and scientific Communism and directed a pedagogical institute. Mikhail Zimyanin was deputy foreign minister and served as ambassador to North Vietnam and Czechoslovakia.

The careers of the *Pravda* chief editors' American counterparts, A. M. Rosenthal, executive editor of *The New York Times*, and Ben Bradlee, executive editor of *The Washington Post*, are markedly different. Rosenthal was a Pulitzer prize-winning foreign correspondent and innovative metropolitan editor; Bradlee served as a *Newsweek* Washington correspondent and bureau chief.

With all important posts filled by the Party, with *Pravda* setting the line, with the Central Committee deciding on circulation and the boss heading the union, there would seem to be little left to chance in the world of the Soviet media. That is not the Party view. Its controls are imposed on three levels: constant interaction between the editorial employees and the *instruktori*, or specialists, of the Central Committee propaganda department; regular meetings of editors with this Central Committee branch; and the final check of the censors, who formally work for Glavlit, a government body, but are widely believed to be under the control of the Central Committee's media experts.[4] A fourth and informal, although greatly effective, control is self-censorship. It could be argued that the three other kinds of control are aimed ultimately at achieving the fourth.

The Central Committee assigns monitors to the national publications and broadcast outlets, whose roles are roughly analogous to those of publishers and station owners in the West. The monitors consult with the editors on ideology and content; in case of dispute, the Central Committee can be appealed to. Lower-level Party specialists maintain liaison in the newsrooms. All

---

4. For a detailed account, see Rand's *The Media and Intra-Elite Communication in the USSR*.

these relationships are duplicated, at a lower level, for republic, regional, and local media. Personnel selection, the *nomenklatura*, has its order of rank as well. The Politburo selects the editor of *Pravda;* the Party secretariat the editors immediately below that level; the Central Committee departments (usually propaganda, but for specialized journals, the departments supervising science or economics) the next lower rank; and finally, as with the monitors, the Republic, district, and city Party organizations.

At all these levels, there are regular meetings between the editors and those in the Party concerned with what is printed and broadcast. Editors of the thirty or so nationally circulated newspapers meet regularly with the Central Committee propaganda department to hear criticism of their work, receive approval for successful campaigns, and learn about new plans to use the press to advance Party goals. The Moscow meetings are held every two or three weeks. A crisis, domestic or international, will produce more frequent meetings.

As described by a former Soviet editor, these meetings could be labeled no-news conferences, the antithesis of a Western news conference. All the normal ingredients of news are there: an issue to be discussed, the Party experts who work with the press present and ready to discuss it, and officials from Party and government to conduct briefings. Often cabinet ministers take part, along with KGB representatives, economists, and experts from the government institutes. The situation—what would normally be a news event—is described in full detail. If there has been an international incident involving the Soviet Union, the views of the USSR's adversary are made known, as well as the official line. If some economic reversal is the topic, honest figures are disclosed. The real casualties from a crash or natural disaster are reported. Ministers and KGB men submit to questioning. It is a journalist's dream.

And then the editors, so carefully briefed and so full of inside knowledge, are told that they are not to print or broadcast a word or a hint of what they have been told, except in a formulation to be worked out by the Party media specialists and handed down to them in a sanitized version carefully prepared and transmitted by TASS.

But the no-news conference goes beyond this simple blanking out. Often, if the situation being discussed is serious enough, a substitute news campaign is launched to get people thinking about other things. The defection of a ballet star or an athlete could be the signal for a series of stories the papers must run about the scandals among ballet stars or athletes in the West, with no mention of the defection, or such veiled mention that only a few insiders would understand the allusion. Food shortages in the Ukraine produce stories about bread lines in Detroit (mention of domestic lines is one of the many thousands of topics banned by the censors).

At other times the no-news conference results in the disappearance of a country or a region for a time. If Russia's relations with West Germany deteriorate over a border incident or a trade deal, and the leadership has not yet decided whether the press should start an anti-German campaign, the solution might be simply to drop all mention of things German for a month or so. To careful readers, these disappearing nations are helps to anticipating policy changes. Argentina's absence from a list of South American nations routinely denounced for being ruled by military dictators was a signal to some insiders that Argentine grain would replace American supplies withheld in the boycott that followed the invasion of Afghanistan, according to a former foreign desk editor. Support for Basque separatist leaders, including free trips to Moscow, showed other readers that after decades of denouncing the Franco dictatorship in Spain, Moscow was disillusioned with the democratic government that replaced it, perhaps because of the poor showing of the Spanish Communists at the polls.

During a period when the emigration of Soviet Jews was reduced to a trickle, and there were widespread reports in the West about official reprisals and harassment of those Jews seeking to leave the country, TASS and *Literaturnaya Gazeta* printed attacks on anti-Semitism—in the United States. An article by Samuil Zivs, the Jewish law professor who heads the government-sponsored Anti-Zionist Committee, brought out some standard anti-Semitic arguments in deploring the situation of American Jews. Anti-Semitism is "organic to the American way of life," he wrote in the paper. "It objectively bears a class character and is aimed against the majority of Jewish American working people. Naturally, anti-Semitism does not affect rich Jews." American anti-Semites, TASS said, "act with the knowledge, and sometimes under the patronage, of American authorities."

Soviet journalists met the challenge of 1984, the year of worldwide publicity for George Orwell's book, with many articles implicitly rejecting the widely held belief that Orwell was describing Soviet or other Communist societies. Not so, these writers said—Orwell was writing about the United States. Soviet readers had to take their word for it; 1984 is banned in the USSR.

The no-news policy is no inconvenience to those of sufficient Party rank to be supplied with the confidential reports that supply honest accounts of events at home and abroad. Ordinary Soviet citizens must cope with heavy jamming if they try to get their news from foreign broadcasts. Privileged citizens are given a monitoring report assembled by KGB technicians whose receivers are located out of the range of jamming. In addition to the TASS service received and printed by Soviet newspapers, there are confidential services available only to a restricted number of officials. Paul Lendvai, who used to prepare such copy for Hungarian officials when he worked for the MTI news agency in Budapest, says more TASS correspondents write for the restricted services than for the general one.[5] According to Lendvai, the most widely circulated special service is the blue TASS, which contains general foreign news, devoid of anti-Soviet statements. Next comes the white TASS, with more complete information, including news about difficulties in the Communist bloc, and the red, which goes only to the top echelon of the leadership and has a commensurately higher index of frankness. Lendvai estimates that no more than 1,000 to 1,500 copies of the white and red TASS are circulated. Soviet journalists now in the West say that ordinary reporters, including some who covered sensitive government affairs, never got to see even the blue TASS, although their editors

---

5. In his book, *The Bureaucracy of Truth* (Boulder, CO: Westview, 1981; London: Burnett Books, 1981).

would sometimes quote to them from it. At one paper, the service was kept in a locked file, and had to be signed out. Lendvai, now a correspondent for the *Financial Times* of London, was once told by a Soviet colleague: "It's easier to get a dacha or a chauffeur-driven car than the red TASS."

The journalistic talents of TASS correspondents are often maligned by their Western colleagues, but there is evidence that their contributions to the restricted services reflect good reporting and propaganda-free writing. A TASS executive once told a Western colleague that the stories his correspondents filed from abroad often contained so much confidential information that they had to be cleared by the Party before they could be circulated in the special TASS services.

Some Soviet journalists now in the West say they were able to provide ordinary readers with information just as good as that in the specialized TASS services, although to extract it took considerable skill at reading between the lines. Skill at writing between-the-lines messages, too, as a former *Komsomolskaya Pravda* reporter explained: "The first part of your article must be about what is being done well. The second part can be about what *will* be done well. The last few lines may be devoted to some constructive criticism, if the language is vague enough." He cited an important pipeline construction project where four or five days of work were being lost every month. Since many of the workers there were young, his paper, organ of the youth organization, sent him there to find the problem. It was drunkenness; on the two paydays every month and for a day or two after, everyone bought vodka and disappeared. The code for this in his report was "problems of scheduling and shift work are being worked out to reduce manpower losses." He admitted that he was careful not to put much of even this heavily veiled kind of criticism in his stories out of concern that he would lose the chance to travel on further assignments.

News parceled out according to rank, timid attempts to circumvent the censors, editors subservient to Party and government: none of this adds up to a very satisfactory press in Western eyes, even the eyes of Western governments. But in the Soviet view, the nation's journalists are doing their job just about right. The

West may need the relentless work of investigative journalists, Soviet editors say, but that is because there are so many differences between the rulers and the ruled. In the USSR, where these conflicts have long ago been laid to rest, it is logical and natural for journalists, as heirs of Lenin, founder of the Soviet press, to share the goals of the government without exception.

The media's role in the Soviet system has firm foundations in Lenin's writing, although it departs in significant ways from some of the tenets of Marxism. As with every other contradiction in Soviet life, this can be explained, and there are many journalists and officials ready to do so. Marx abhorred censorship; the Soviet Union has multiple layers of censors controlling everything that is printed or otherwise made public, from encyclopedias to wedding invitations. One way of dealing with this contradiction is to explain that Marx was talking about a different society and completely different conditions. He opposed the censorship that kept radical views from reaching the readers of the dominant bourgeois press of the nineteenth century. In the Soviet Union, the radicals are supposed to be in charge, and since the people have chosen to have only one party, the Communist, it would be senseless to permit its press to air the views of other parties and factions.

Another way of dealing with Marx is to censor him. Marx's best-known words on the topic, "a censored press remains bad even when it produces good things," cannot be found in print in the Soviet Union.[6] The quotation could be looked up by those with access to the closed-shelf sections of the Lenin library in Moscow (where entire years of *Pravda* are also kept, since they mention Trotsky, Bukharin, and other purge victims). It must also be on file in the offices of the censorship agency, Glavlit, but that, too, would be hard for a researcher to trace, since the existence of Glavlit is information censored from the public.

In Leninism, the authoritarian structure built on top of Marxism to make it an easier system of ruling a backward country, there are clear elements that help explain why the Soviet media act the

---

6. As noted by John Karch in *Comparative Mass Media Systems* (L. John Martin and Anju Chaudhary. New York: Longman, Inc., 1983).

way they do, and indeed could do little else. The principles with the most direct application are democratic centralism, *partiinost*, and the role of the Party as surrogate for the masses.

To start with the third point, Lenin maintained that the Party, the minority, was there to guide the majority, the workers. This heavy-handed guidance has remained a central function of the present-day Party. Marx had thought the conditions the working class of his time lived under gave it a special revolutionary consciousness that eventually would equip it to lead. Lenin contended that, unguided, the workers were interested only in improving their economic lot. They needed the Communists, vanguard of the proletariat, to lead them. The only thing to add was the trappings of worker participation. The media reflect this Party guidance of the masses in many ways. White-collar editors send white-collar journalists to write about the problems of the production line and construction site. White-collar photographers fill the papers and television programs with portraits of craggy-faced miners and Central Asian weavers in traditional headgear. But factory workers who have tried to use the media themselves to draw attention to safety hazards or inequities in pay and workloads report they are brushed aside by editors, unless their complaints happen to coincide with some campaign launched from on high.

Partiinost, or partisanship, expresses Lenin's view that all knowledge reflects the ideology of one class or another; there can be no such thing as neutrality or objectivity. But only the Communists' ideology is correct, since it represents the working class—all other classes' ideologies are wrong, and so, therefore, are the ideas produced by those under their influence. "The talk of absolute freedom is only a disguise," Lenin wrote. His successors add: "Socialist literature and art have demonstrated, as Lenin predicted, that true freedom exists in serving the masses." For journalists, serving the masses means not only abandoning objectivity but supporting the Party in plans and decisions that may seem absolutely stupid but cannot be wrong.

Democratic centralism was Lenin's way of coping with the Marxist view that the dominant feature of a classless society should be democracy. Democracy was difficult to maintain under conditions of revolution and civil war, the Leninists argued, and when those conditions passed, there was always another reason to put it off: industrialization, collectivizing agriculture, the rise of Fascism, the war, postwar reconstruction, the Cold War. Democratic centralism permits both a show of democracy and a tight ship. It is supposed to permit free discussion of controversies in Party bodies until a decision is made, and, after that, iron discipline in carrying out the decision without question. Over the decades, the discussion phase of democratic centralism atrophied and the discipline strengthened. Decisions were presented readymade to the Party councils supposedly empowered to make those decisions. To question such a decision meant expulsion from those councils, and, in Stalin's time, far worse. Only the centralism remained: Party members carrying out the policies and instructions that had been formulated without their participation by the center.

The effect of these and other strictures on the media can be observed every day: they are guided, censored, and written by the Party; they argue Party views on the comfortable basis that the Party can do no wrong; and finally, they brook no real criticism or opposition, since what appears in print or is broadcast already has approval on high. The news on *"Vremya"* and the opinions in *Pravda*, in short, represent decisions of the leadership that cannot be challenged.

Such demands might seem to set impossible standards of performance for fallible men and women reporting and writing about a huge country with huge problems. In practice, they and their editors cope with their burden of responsibility the way other cogs in the machinery of the Soviet system do: they play it safe, pass tricky decisions upward or to the censors, and have the assurance, finally, that there is no competing newspaper or station that might get the real story or point out shortcomings in their performance.

There are no competing media at home, but sometimes it is possible to assess Soviet journalists' and editors' performance in comparison to that of their colleagues in the West. Convenient and informative occasions for comparison are the recurrent Soviet invasions of neighboring countries.

In 1956, Wilbur Schramm, at that time at Stanford, drew up a comparison of how fourteen of the world's leading newspapers covered international and domestic news. Schramm and a staff of translators compared *Pravda, The New York Times,* the *Times* of London, *Le Monde,* the *Frankfurter Allgemeine,* and nine other papers of November 2. That was the day British, French, and Israeli troops were preparing to invade Egypt, which had nationalized the Suez Canal, and Soviet troops returned to Hungary in force to crush that nation's fight for independence.

The Suez situation, a threat to world peace, got the top billing in the world's press, with Hungary a close second in most papers. The Suez story was also easier to cover; a stream of announcements was pouring from the four key capitals. Moscow was saying nothing about Hungary, and the chaos in Budapest made it almost impossible to get reliable information. Some papers, like the *Frankfurter Allgemeine,* gave both stories about equal play. One, *Dagens Nyheter* of Stockholm, devoted more space to Hungary than to Suez. *The New York Times* gave Suez nearly nine times the wordage it did Hungary; most papers' ratios were about six to one.

For *Pravda,* the ratio was forty to one: a total of 262 column inches on Suez and only six inches on the crisis in its own backyard. The Suez stories, beginning with a banner headline, HANDS OFF EGYPT!, fill the pages of the paper. The dispatch about Hungary is only about one hundred words, and it occupies an inconspicuous spot on the back page. Filed by TASS from Budapest, it starts out like this: "On the night of October 31, all was quiet in Budapest."

Soviet troops were on the move again in the final days of December 1979, this time into Afghanistan. A comparison of coverage between *Pravda* and *The New York Times* shows no change in the intervening twenty-three years in Moscow's obligation to inform its people about international actions that would seriously affect them.

The *Times* lead item on December 27 was headlined U.S. RE-

PORTS SOVIET FLYING MANY TROOPS TO AFGHAN CONFLICT. The Washington dispatch said U.S. officials had reported that "in the last 24 hours the Soviet Union had begun a round-the-clock airlift to Afghanistan, raising Soviet military involvement in that country to 'a new threshold.'"

Pravda's main story on December 27 was headlined BASIS FOR GROWTH OF INDUSTRY. On an inside page, it had a two-paragraph dispatch from its correspondent, L. Mironov, reporting that the ruling Afghan People's Democratic Party had observed its fifteenth anniversary.

The New York Times' three-column headline the following day, December 28, had more interesting political news from Kabul: AFGHAN PRESIDENT IS OUSTED AND EXECUTED IN KABUL COUP, RE-PORTEDLY WITH SOVIET HELP. *Pravda*'s lead story that day was headlined STRENGTHENING LEGALITY AND JUSTICE, and it dealt with the new Soviet constitution. Inside, in the middle of the foreign news page, there was a TASS dispatch quoting Kabul radio on the coup and the deposing of President Amin, who, it turned out, had been an agent of American imperialism all along.

The next day, events in Iran pushed Afghanistan from the lead spot in the *Times,* and *Pravda* continued to use its front page for congratulations to workers and praise of construction projects. Deep inside, there was a short TASS dispatch about an Afghan appeal to the Soviet Union for "immediate political, moral, and economic aid, including military aid." With its armored divisions already fighting in Afghanistan, the Soviet Union acknowledged laconically that the request had been granted.

When the College of Cardinals chose Karol Wojtyla to be the first Polish pope and the first non-Italian to hold the post in centuries, the news filled the papers and the airwaves of much of the world for many days. All across Europe, Eastern as well as Western, there were thousands of stories about Wojtyla's background, the course the Vatican would take, the new pope's thoughts about every topic from religion to the Third World.

In the Soviet Union, *Pravda* ran a two-paragraph news item on its foreign page: The first paragraph reported that the Vatican had chosen a new pope; the second identified him as "Karol Wojtyla of Poland." The editors of the *Current Digest of the Soviet Press* could find no other reference to the event in more than two weeks of scanning Soviet newspapers.

It is easy to keep track of the Soviet media's omissions in accounts of important international events, since so many other sources of information from outside the country are available. We can only guess at the amount of domestic news that must go unreported because it would reflect unfavorably on those able to control the press at the local or national level. Western analysts who keep track of plan and production figures can tell when goals are not met or figures falsified; Western correspondents have a way of learning about scandals that would otherwise go unreported and of following up on the political meaning of the personnel changes announced without explanation in obscure little articles in *Pravda*.

But there are great areas of Soviet life, such as working conditions, dangerous or simply dreary, that do not get reported on at all in the domestic or the foreign press. The country is too vast, and its officials too adept at concealing their inability to cope with the quality-of-life problems almost every Soviet citizen experiences: food and consumer goods shortages, inadequacies in housing, day care, and transportation.

"I have been sent out on many such assignments, investigating complaints brought to our editors' attention by letter writers," a journalist who works for a major Party daily said. "Often we have been able to see the results in improved local conditions." He conceded, however, that reporting on complaints from factories and other state enterprises was made more difficult because the manager's permission must first be obtained. It can be imagined that managers are reluctant to open their doors to inquiring reporters, even if they believe all are members of the same pro-government team. If the next higher level of management has an interest in what may be going wrong at the enterprise, it can intervene and force the local manager to let the journalist investigate the complaints.

Reporters sent to follow up reader complaints agree that it is easier to gain access to municipal officials than to those of the state economy, and easier to produce results. The stock in trade of the local reader complaint is the overcrowded apartment or lack of services. Someone can usually be prodded into action in fixing the ubiquitous leaking roof or in determining if the complainant has been unfairly treated on waiting lists for new apartments.

If this sounds like the kind of service to readers that any well-run small newspaper in the West does, it is important to remember the differences. Journalists do not initiate these modest efforts at investigative reporting; they are told by the editors what complaints to follow and what not to follow. The editors, in turn, are usually cued by the city or regional authorities in Party and government. A few journalists can recall editors strong and independent enough to make their own decisions on some matters of local controversy, but their strength came from good connections higher up.

An equally important difference is that the reporters would not dare go beyond the local symptoms of what are often basic national problems—the housing shortage, for one. An afternoon of research would show any enterprising journalist what part of the national budget in Western countries goes for housing and what part for armaments, and how this compares to Soviet priorities. But, in the highly unlikely event that such findings could ever be printed in any form other than the *samizdat* of the dissident underground, it would be an afternoon that would lead directly to the labor camps on charges of anti-Soviet propaganda and agitation or dozens of other possible accusations. And the roofs would continue to leak.

Of course, even the most courageous Soviet journalists do not risk frontal attacks. One method that sometimes succeeds is humor; the regime likes to laugh, or at least smile, at itself. Satirical columns and the satirical magazine *Krokodil* are popular with readers. Much of the satire is directed at the West, moreover, although careful readers can detect a point being made against practices at home from time to time. Despite their popularity, satirists are the most vulnerable of Soviet journalists to official criticism and frequently to dismissal or transfer to other writing duties.

A contributor to a regional daily in the Ukraine said he found ideas everywhere for his humor column: unfinished construction projects; environmental damage; trains, planes, and buses that never arrived on schedule or on which seats were commandeered by officials; and, of course, the housing shortage. Joking about these conditions took some of the bite out of the criticism but left the point in, he said. But after a time, columns that had been passed and even praised by his editor were rejected for publication at the last minute. There did not seem to be any logic behind the rejection, he said: a piece that he thought was completely innocuous would be turned down, another one that he thought might have gone too far would be published. In neither case was he ever able to get any guidance or explanation. His conclusion was that Party interference over the head of the editor was to blame, but that the Party operatives had no real feel for what constituted dangerous criticism and what did not. The effect of their interventions, however, was to persuade the satirist to seek another line of safer journalistic work.

His newspaper, of course, lost a bright and original column, and his readers lost another reason for picking up the paper from newsstands. Although the brightly written *Literaturnaya Gazeta* is an exception, attracting readers does not seem to be a very high-priority item for Soviet editors. The Soviet press is dull and unadventurous for the same reasons government publicity handouts are. In both cases, texts have been hedged and revised many times by cautious bureaucrats oblivious to good writing and concerned with concealment rather than revelation.

The Party considers literature, art, and drama as much a part of its apparatus for informing and persuading as it does newspapers and broadcasts, and the hand of the censor weighs as heavily on creative artists as it does on journalists. As with the journalists, there are courageous men and women who try to resist writing literature that serves the masses. Their task is easier in some ways and harder in others. Literature can be written for the drawer and future publication; journalism must be current. But journalism, on the other hand, is a group effort where it is more difficult to crack down on individuals. The literary writer is alone and exposed.

Seven decades of Soviet literature have been seven decades of literary warfare between writers and rulers. Even those writers who did not support the revolution expected better conditions than they had experienced under the czars. The Russian symbolists and futurists thought they would find sympathy from a regime that also characterized itself as avant-garde. They soon discovered that political and artistic revolutions were entirely different matters. Lenin understood and controlled the former; he did not understand and was suspicious of the latter. He admired Tolstoy, but as a journalist, not a writer. Tolstoy's novels portrayed nineteenth-century Russian society so richly and accurately that twentieth-century readers could almost feel they had experienced it. In postrevolutionary Russia, the Party sought the twentieth-century Tolstoys to portray contemporary society. But it was a portrayal narrow rather than sweeping and broad that was wanted: "A vivid and convincing reflection of new human personalities, new social relations, and the problems of building a communist society."

There was clearly no place in this scheme for writers who experimented with language and form, who ridiculed the stuffy official or Party zealot, who chronicled the individual tragedies that accompanied collectivization or the rush to industrialize.

It took the regime little more than a decade to tame the writers. The suicide of Vladimir Mayakovsky, the adored proletarian poet, in 1930, marked the end of the period of tolerance and the beginning of the era of literature in the service of the state. "It isn't easy to clean out/ the bureaucratic swarm. There aren't enough baths /Nor is there soap enough . . ." Mayakovsky had written in the last year of his life.

But as long as the censors could be held back, the young Soviet state experienced a richness of literary creativity comparable in many ways to the great years of the nineteenth and early twentieth century. Eugene Zamyatin's novel *We*, written in 1920, anticipated both *Brave New World* and *1984*. It is the twenty-ninth century, and the collective "we" has replaced the individual "I." After a two-hundred-year war, everyone lives in a city called the Only State, with numbers instead of names and a glass wall to protect them from the unorganized world of nature outside. *We* had to be published abroad, and has never appeared officially in the Soviet Union. One of the characters in Yuri Olesha's *Envy* is a New Soviet Man who envies the precision of machines and wants to become one. Boris Pilnyak, who considered his 1920 book, *The Bare Years*, the first Soviet novel, wrote of the struggle between the ways of old Russia and the "leather jackets," the Communist organizers who wanted to make everything rational and mechanized. Mikhail Zoshchenko has a barely literate character in one of his books who speaks in snippets of officialese and news stories.

When Stalin outlawed nonconformist literature in the 1930s, all four of these innovators suffered. Pilnyak wrote propaganda and then disappeared in the purges. Zamyatin went abroad. Olesha published nothing for twenty years. Zoshchenko was expelled from the writers' union. But their works are still read, in the West and in secret in the East, long after people have forgotten the writers who replaced them and wrote to please the Party.

As with the press, the official literature lost the vital quality of honesty that writers had been able to maintain even under the imperial censors. If a state tries to decree what its writers may not write, as the Czarist state did, that is bad enough, but here was a state able to dictate what would be written.

Tolstoy's realism was replaced by Socialist Realism, defined by a Stalin-era writers' congress as truthful, historically concrete writing "linked with the task of ideological transformation and education of workers in the spirit of socialism." Since the spirit of socialism is optimistic and forward-looking, so is Socialist Realism. Andrei Sinyavsky once compiled a list of the titles of Western and Soviet novels. He compared *Death in the Afternoon* and *Journey to the End of the Night* to Bagritsky's *The Victors*, Simonov's *The Victor*, and a whole series of similar titles.

As Edward Brown, the American critic, says, "Socialist Realism is supposed to be a barometer of society, but the Soviet authorities have tried to rig it so that it would always be on fair. Its departures from verisimilitude are anti-human. It uses pessimism, even sex, only as an index of the decline of society; the absence of those two elements is seen as positive."

What results are characters, narrative passages, chapters, and entire volumes that seem as wooden and written to a formula as the worst pulp westerns. This is pulp, moreover, that is not only put forward as the mainstream literature of a nation with a great literary tradition, but as the only literature. Some short samples may suffice. A war veteran on his way to lead a brass band that will play at the unveiling of a war memorial is offered a drink from some of the younger band members. "No, boys," he answers (firmly). "You do as you please, but I won't breathe vodka into my mouthpiece. I have to play the National Anthem today." A cosmonaut improbably rescued from a forced landing in Siberia by a gruff old forester is received as a hero by the press, officials, and cheering crowds, but he has his private thoughts: "Will we be able to keep that goodness of heart into our old age, or will we let silly trivialities get the better of us? Aren't we mechanizing ourselves and our feelings?"

The war veteran and the cosmonaut are positive heroes, the Soviet replacement for the nineteenth century's superfluous hero. Pushkin's Eugene Onegin was such a hero. He's never sure he's doing the right thing. He doesn't march confidently to the future; he stumbles.

Heroes in Soviet literature stopped doing that in the 1930s. This is not to say that everyone in novels and plays since then has been a positive character. There are negative people, too, but at least it's plain—painfully plain—where they stand.

The superfluous hero, Sinyavsky wrote, was more suspect than the clearcut negative enemy, since the latter was "like the positive hero . . . straightforward, and in his own way, purposeful." The superfluous man couldn't be pinned down: "He is neither for the Purpose nor against the Purpose—he is outside the Purpose." Such figures were not needed. "There were no heroes without Purpose but only heroes who were for or against the Purpose . . . the superfluous hero was, when all is said and done, a camouflaged enemy."

Adhering to this formula of clear black and white is a guarantee of success in Soviet writing. There must be some conflict, of course; otherwise there would be no plot. The positive hero takes control of the situation, brings in the harvest, builds the dam, beats the Germans, thwarts the CIA. Most importantly, he or she teaches readers a lesson in the process of overcoming adversity that they may find useful in their own lives.

"Write this way, and do it with halfway intelligence, and your career is assured," a widely published writer who has refused offers of exile in the West said. Those who try to bend the rules to just the right degree, men like Valentin Rasputin and the late Yuri Trifonov, are the most successful, since the public will swallow the didactic elements in them to get to the social criticism and literary quality. Those who produce industrial novels, in which both content and creation are production-oriented, sell in the millions but do not have the artistic satisfaction of the bolder writers, he said.

Into this placid world dropped a former Soviet artillery captain, Alexander Solzhenitsyn, released from the Gulag with a self-imposed mission of settling the score with Stalinism. No writer and no theme could be further removed from the world of the industrial novel. Solzhenitsyn was an individual in a system that discourages individuality. In his case, it was the system of the camps that produced the individuality. If the same conditions also produced his arrogance, readers have the right to ignore the second and treasure the first.

Solzhenitsyn restored the superfluous hero to Soviet literature, as well as some of the real language. Socialist Realist writing is flat and preachy compared to his. He writes of camps, villages, and hospitals, a compressed version of what is happening in the larger Soviet society outside. Life isn't perfect, and it isn't even assured of becoming perfect, as in the officially sanctioned literature. It's bearable, though, in large part because of the individuals who pass through his stories, human, believable.

The main quality is honesty. Much of Solzhenitsyn's work was written without any hope at the time of being published. That freed him from the self-censorship and equivocation about taking risks that other Soviet writers must deal with.

Solzhenitsyn was able to take advantage of a temporary set of conditions—the post-Stalin thaw and Nikita Khrushchev's interest in using revelations about Stalin's years to battle the Old Guard. He also had the advantage of a strong editor at *Novy Mir,*

Alexander Tvardovsky, his own limitless courage, and his resourcefulness in hiding manuscripts from the KGB and pressing for their publication. Those conditions meant that for a time, there was an uncompromisingly honest voice among Soviet writers. Now it is heard only from abroad.

Some of those same conditions made it possible for Yuri Lyubimov, the theater director later forced into exile, to put on stage a frankly critical view of Soviet society (although one set comfortably in the past). *The House on the Embankment*, based on a Trifonov novella, dealt with betrayal by the secret police and the effects of Stalinism on families, something Trifonov knew from his own life. But Lyubimov was thwarted by the censors many times for each such triumph, and the general run of plays on the nation's stages, not surprisingly, is as mundane as the literature in print.

Theaters, as state industries, work on a plan. Major theaters must stage four new productions a year: one patriotic, one contemporary, one historic/classic, and one foreign. The patriotic is usually a World War II drama in which the Soviet side (as it did in fact) wins, credit goes to the Communists, who rally the people, and a lesson is taught. Often the theme is the revolution or civil war; the Afghanistan war still awaits its stage chronicler. The historic/classical is easy, since Russian playwrights were filling the stages of the world before the revolution. Foreign plays are dealt with gingerly. It was considered daring for a Leningrad theater to produce *Cat on a Hot Tin Roof* in 1981. The contemporary plays stress the need for patriotism and building socialism through individual sacrifice and group effort.

The acting and directing are often markedly better than the material; one great advantage of a state theater is the schools and training stages where artists study their craft from early childhood.

What does the theater bring the public besides the messages the regime wants communicated? An American diplomat whose job it was to monitor culture said that after a year of theater-going in Moscow and the provinces he could not point to a single performance that really dealt with the problems of everyday life in a realistic way. Playwrights, he said, were simply not being permitted to fulfill one of their functions as artists, to explain the human condition with the hope of making life more liveable, or perhaps to induce pressure for change. Instead, there were grand themes and cardboard heroes and heroines.

Contemporary opera sets the cardboard to music, to judge from a sampling of the new works tucked among the first-rate productions of the classics in four Soviet cities. On one notable evening, battles were being fought against German negative heroes on the stage to the accompaniment of mildly dissonant music while the audience struggled with decisions to stay or go home. By the first intermission, a good one-fourth had departed. By the second, it was half, and when the final curtain went down, the bulk of the audience was made up of World War II veterans in blue serge suits, with the rainbow patterns of ribbons and medals on their chests.

The same patriotic tableaux can be seen inside gold frames in the nation's galleries and in the bright colors of posters on building walls. The propaganda poster and painting was used to get across ideas the printed word could not because of the high illiteracy rate in the first years after the revolution. Those early works are still on view in some museums. They do not look much different from what is produced for the literate 1980s.

In Lvov, in the Ukraine, there is a whole school of collective farm art, showing private farmers the advantages of joining the collective. Hard-working peasant families are depicted gaping in wonder at the new collective tractors moving easily through the fields of grain. The parallels with contemporary television are striking. In Uzbekistan, the old posters show backward-looking Muslims exploiting women, but the clean-cut Uzbek Communists, wearing only token parts of the national dress, are steering people on the right path, away from oppression and superstition. The same characters appear in different costumes in other parts of the Soviet Union to attack Russian Orthodox clergymen. The Orthodox clergymen have stolen money from the people; the Muslim imams sheep.

The poster industry is still in full swing, and the themes are little changed. An artist in a poster studio in a provincial city explained that seven people work on painting and silk-screening posters, which are produced on the basis of a short-term and a long-term plan so that anniversaries are taken care of but Party campaigns introduced at relatively short notice can also be accommodated. There are fifteen such shops in the city, she said. Some specialize in banners, and two sculptors work almost full time on statues of Communist heroes and monuments. The most popular banners are the shortest: "Long Live the Great Soviet People" or "Long Live Communism," since Party specialists think those are positive messages, easy to absorb. The artist seemed less enthusiastic about her job than were the people on the cheerful posters she produced extolling labor. She was really there in the hope of being able to work someday as a real painter, she confided, much as someone in her position on Madison Avenue might.

In addition to its poster and banner industry, the USSR has a higher level of officially produced art. Painters of this genre belong to the artists' union and are on government salaries. They know that their work has a life span of about ten years, after which it will be removed from museums and stored or perhaps burned. This is done to make way for another series of scenes from the history of the revolution, the life of Lenin, or the successes of Soviet industry. These artists accept the limitations of a life of painting coking ovens, or Wehrmacht tanks being blown up by Red Army artillery. They are guaranteed a much higher standard of living than are the unofficial artists, who must live from their sales, find it hard to buy paint and materials, and are seldom exhibited. Even this unofficial art, or that exhibited officially in easy-going places like Soviet Armenia, is hardly startling by Western standards. Much of it is reminiscent of 1930s modernism; nudes are a rarity much commented on.

The rest is pure Socialist Realism, and as the crowds walk through the galleries, they seem to appreciate the scenes from their lives and from the more stirring times they have heard and read about. (The rare Picasso on display provokes titters of disbelief.) One of the favorite kinds of portraits are the group pictures of the leadership, somber men in dark suits against somber walls and furniture, in the manner of the court paintings of old.

The paint-and-burn school of art has its advantages in a nation where leaders often disappear from public mention after they die or are forced out of office. A Soviet Mount Rushmore would have only one carved face, Lenin's, with blanked-out spaces for Stalin, Malenkov, and Khrushchev, where carving had been removed, and scaffolding and tarpaulins covering the Brezhnev, Andropov, and Chernenko sections while officials delayed the cutting for a while.

There are similar blank spaces in every Soviet historical account. John Reed's *Ten Days that Shook the World* might seem to be safe from censorship. Reed is buried in the Kremlin wall; Lenin called the book a "truthful and most vivid exposition" of the events that brought the Bolsheviks to power. Western critics consider Reed's 1919 work too partisan, but Reed, an American radical who became a Comintern official, made no apologies for his views. The Western criticism is kind compared to the Soviet.

Stalin banned the book. It reappeared in the Khrushchev era, with long explanations to readers who may have been puzzled why Reed called men like Trotsky, Zinoviev, and Kamenev heroes of the revolution when Stalin ordered them executed as traitors.

The explanations were dropped from a 1981 edition for tenth-grade Soviet classes in English. So were Trotsky and the other purge victims. Trotsky's absence is particularly awkward, because of his central role in the revolution. It's like a history of the American civil war without General Grant, but the Soviet censors proved up to the task.

In the original version, for example, Reed ends an account of a key battle with a triumphant telegram announcing the victory of Bolshevik forces over those of the provisional Kerensky government. "The night of October 30th will go down in history," the telegram says. Not in the 1981 version, it won't. The entire passage is simply chopped out. The chapter ends with a limp scene about promises to reopen the railroads. The reason is that the victory was won by forces commanded by Leon Trotsky, and the telegram Reed quoted was written and signed by him.

The censors make dozens of changes in other parts of the text to erase the latter part of the "Lenin and Trotsky" phrases. "That the Bolsheviki would remain in power longer than three days never occurred to anybody—except perhaps to Lenin . . . the Petrograd workers, and the soldiers," the tenth-graders read. The ellipsis stands for Trotsky.

Reed's rewriters polish the reputation of Lenin as they eliminate his lieutenants, and they prettify accounts of the chaos of revolution. In one passage, Lenin is shouted down in a meeting of peasants not yet ready to join his revolution. Reed original: "Lenin suddenly mounted the tribune; for ten minutes the room went mad. 'Down with him!' they shrieked. 'We will not listen to any of your People's Commissars!'" Censored version: "Lenin suddenly appeared on the tribune; for ten minutes the room went mad. 'Down with him! We will not listen to any of your People's Commissars!' some of the reactionary delegates cried."

Reed writes of soldiers breaking windows to storm a train he was riding on. In the new version, they simply crowded aboard. Reed tells of the railroad unions' initial opposition to Lenin, and explains its causes. Since today's unions can't oppose anything, that part is dropped. Reed writes of "gold and colored spires and cupolas, with heightened barbaric splendor." The censors cut out both the barbarism and the splendor. Long passages about power struggles in the Party, massacres committed by Bolsheviks, and some of the other ugly scenes of the revolution are simply left out.

The Soviet censors do not want Reed to detract from the nobility of the workers and soldiers who made the revolution. They are not confident enough, seven decades later, to be able to approve a candid account of a very violent period in their nation's past. If Soviet officialdom cannot yet admit that an occasional soldier, worker, or Bolshevik leader did wrong, it is not surprising that the world still awaits an honest history from a Soviet writer who is not in the ranks of the exiles.

Grigory Gurevich is a slim, elegant man in his early forties whose experiences embody every facet of Soviet restrictions on intellectual life and creativity. Gurevich learned the limitations imposed on journalism, theater, art, and free expression in a career that spanned two decades in the Soviet Union. He talks about it these days in a brownstone duplex crowded with prints, paintings, and theater posters on a Jersey City side street. As architect, designer, poet, artist, and mime, Gurevich experienced success when quite young, but it was always counterpoised by the official limitations on what he could create.

He learned of the power of the press to dictate opinion soon after finishing his studies in architecture and design. His graduation project was a modern chair, with seat and back supports strung with stout cord in the fashion of a harp or suspension bridge. The white cord contrasted nicely with black wrought-iron legs and frames, and the chair looked as though it might have been imported from one of the famous Scandinavian workshops.

But to the Leningrad youth newspaper *Smena*, it looked un-Russian. *Smena*, in a short article on the graduation exhibit, singled out Gurevich and wondered why he hadn't designed something more in keeping with what Russians were used to having in their homes, rather than something from the West.

Soon afterwards, Gurevich was called to the exhibition. His chair had been ruined—someone had slashed through all his carefully placed cords.

The Soviet Union's upper class were more discerning, and Gurevich made good money designing and outfitting their dachas and apartment interiors. But, in the spirit of the 1960s and the relaxed cultural climate that continued into the early 1970s, he wanted to use his talents in more purposeful ways. He began writing and performing short and biting sketches in a mime troupe, first under Arkady Raikan, the Soviet Union's best comedian, and then on his own. "Raikan is so good and so secure that he can take on anything," Gurevich says. "But when I left to work by myself, I found that it wasn't that easy."

A little of the flavor of Gurevich's mime sketches can be conveyed by the scripts he prepares for them.

Man and Society. A system strives to crush man's free spirit and turn it into a part of itself. Man . . . as soon as he attempts to move freely he encounters the obstacle of the programmed working machine. Trying to break free, he goes out of his mind and turns into a cog of the machine. The next man repeats the course of his

predecessor, but turns out to be stronger. He demol-
ishes the machine and creates a new one.

Gurevich wasn't able to overcome the machinery of censorship
and give regular performances. Occasionally, a small theater
would be available, but after the performance, which culture officials would view in stony silence, he would be told that every
theater in Leningrad was fully booked—something any local the-
atergoer knew was patently untrue. Gurevich was never told that
his themes were too bold, that he couldn't compare the Soviet
system to a machine, much less demolish it and create a better
one. He was simply given excuses. But one day, an official took
him aside and said: "That machine act—that could be about fascism, not Communism. Can't you do something to show that this
is a Soviet creation, not a Western? Privately, between us,
wouldn't it be possible to come out on the stage with a Soviet flag
at some point?"

As an artist, Gurevich encountered the same kind of censorship
by excuse and ambiguity. The basic problem with his work was
that it wasn't representational. He knew that, and the city art
establishment knew that.

To Gurevich, it was not so much a matter of the sales that official approval would guarantee, but of the exposure: "What is
really important is to be able to show your work to others, to be
addressing them when you paint or sculpt or engrave. Without
that, you're talking to yourself." And so he went from committee
to committee, sometimes waiting an entire day in an anteroom to
get a screening and the stamp of approval that would permit him
to exhibit officially.

Instead, he would be told: "These are engravings, and we're
interested in oils right now—we've had too many engraving exhibits lately." Sometimes a member of the committee would tell
him privately that the work really wasn't the kind of thing they
wanted to approve. "It doesn't tell us anything of Soviet reality,"
one functionary told the artist. "It has a Western look."

Gurevich's work seems harmless enough. One favorite theme
is a circular pattern of faintly abstract human bodies in a kind of
pool. It has a pleasant, decorative effect, nothing jarring. What is

wrong, at least for Soviet conditions, is what Gurevich chose not to include. There is no optimism, no expression of the glory of work and accomplishment, no scenes from people's real lives.

"Why don't you conform a little bit?" one member of an artists' union jury asked Gurevich. "Why are you always trying to resist?"

In the middle seventies, when it became possible to emigrate, Gurevich stopped trying to resist, as did thousands of other men and women in the arts and intellectual professions. The cultural life and the media of Western Europe, Israel, and the United States became the richer for it, and that of the Soviet Union, its censorship machinery a little dented but still intact, the poorer.

• 3 •

"A Unique Soviet Form of Public Opinion"

The letters office of the Central Committee of the Communist Party of the Soviet Union looks a little like a branch post office or employment bureau, one of the many places where citizen meets bureaucrat to obtain something, usually after a long wait in line. There are stand-up tables for writing letters, a window for handing them in, another window, on the way to the exit door, to receive a reply or explanation, and chairs to sit on in between. The office, on a downtown Moscow street in a district filled by the Central Committee's headquarters and departments, was set up to provide the Party with two benefits: giving the people assurance that their complaints were being listened to, and finding out, in the process, what their concerns and problems are. In some ways, it is a direct link between ordinary citizens and the most powerful ruling body in the land, one of many means, Soviet officials say, that the people have to address their leaders. But since those same officials are unable to supply information on the results of the three million letters that go through that part of the opinion system each year, it is hard to gauge its effectiveness.

The office is always busy, according to those Western correspondents in Moscow whose Russian is good enough to make it a profitable venue for man- and woman-on-the-street interviews. On one wintry day, about fifty people were writing letters, some laboriously, some with apparent indignation, and one, a little girl wrapped cutely in furs, being indulged by her parents. There was much traffic back and forth in front of the windows, as people talked to the clerks who represent, at least to the petitioners, the power of the Party.

The concerns of the letter writers that day were heavily weighted on the side of the problems that in other societies would be the province of the landlord, the union representative, or the Better Business Bureau: the apartment roof leak, the disappearance of a prized electrical appliance at the repair shop, rudeness at the local butcher's, unfair treatment in sick leave. The Party either promises to help, turns the complainant down, or refers him or her to some other office. Usually the answer is ready the same morning or afternoon that the letter is handed in—an improvement over the old letter slot in the Kremlin wall used by the czars and by Soviet leaders up until Khrushchev's time to receive petitions, but not necessarily to respond to them. Whether the results have improved is difficult to say. In any case, the letter link to the Central Committee seems such a mutually beneficial arrangement to keep contact between the leadership and the people they rule that one wonders why it took so long to work it out.

In the Moscow offices of *Trud*, the Soviet trade union newspaper, so many letters from readers arrive every day that they have to be hauled around in a supermarket shopping cart. *Trud*, the nation's (and the world's) largest daily, with a circulation of fourteen million, gets 600,000 letters a year. Hundreds of thousands of other letters flow to *Pravda*, *Izvestia*, the regional and local newspapers, the republic, regional, and local Party and government offices, and the news departments of the broadcast stations.

As with those addressed to the Central Committee, the letter writing serves the dual purposes of complaint channel and opinion gauge. Despite the massive volume of letters, however, the letter-writing process is only one of many ways to inform the leadership about what is going on in the country.

The government and its institutes commission polls, although they rarely make their results public. There are thousands of regular meetings in factories, apartment blocks, and offices, where officials engage in what are usually one-sided discussions on current events, problems, and Party goals with workers and employees. These workplace meetings are supplemented by others for the general public to discuss domestic or foreign policy issues. Occasionally there will be a nationwide campaign designed to encourage public participation, such as the call for amendments to the 1977 constitution. One main channel of information is provided by the Party itself, local organizations transmitting what is learned at the grass roots to the next higher level, and that level selecting what is important and informing the next.

But one of the barriers to any realistic measurement of public opinion in the Soviet Union is that it is easy, indeed, frequently obligatory, to register approval for something the government is doing but difficult to express even mild disapproval. In a nation where everyone over forty can remember, and can recall with vivid detail for Westerners, what it was like to live in fear of the knock on the door during the years of Stalin, people think twice and often more times than that before letting their opinion be known. "Fear is still the czar in the Soviet Union," an émigré linguist said. Another émigré who had worked at a high level in the Moscow bureaucracy said complaining to the authorities often leads to the complainer's being associated with the problem, and this, too, casts a chill on the open expression of opinion.

Informing on the activities and attitudes of people carries no such stigma. The Soviet Union encourages informers, even making it possible for one citizen to denounce another anonymously by filling out a printed postcard form. Some informers are actuated by Party spirit or a dislike of corruption, according to a Western analyst who interviews hundreds of Soviet citizens when they come to the West. "Others are paid," he said. "Some have something to feel guilty about, and the authorities know it. But most are paid in privileges like apartments or promotions. The desirable apartments in the city centers have to go to somebody—why not to those who volunteer?"

The analyst said his interviews disclose the existence of KGB safe houses, even in small villages, where local agents meet and debrief their informants. Sometimes their information leads to denunciations and arrests, but that is not the only aim of the system, which is designed to cast a broad net for information of all kinds useful to the government. What's the mood like on the big collective farm where they had to replace the chairman? Are the

Soviet soldiers stationed nearby still black-marketing gasoline and canned meat? Is the theft rate at construction sites going above the normally high but tolerable level?

Soviet citizens who have gone through these interviews say that the questioners seem to have independent sources of information. They use what they have learned from other informants to cross-check and keep stories within the bounds of accuracy. The usual stock in trade is a report on a family or personal problem: drinking, theft of state property, fighting, absenteeism. But the sum of these individual stories constitutes a picture of Soviet social ills for anyone wishing to collect and evaluate them for the leadership.

It is easy to see that the picture could get somewhat distorted in the long trip from safe house interview in the provinces to Dzerzhinsky Square in Moscow, and that some stories might never get beyond the local KGB officials. After all, too much black marketing or malingering in a district could look bad for the security people responsible. Informants and agents can be sloppy ("the lazy KGB agent was our real friend," a dissident from Leningrad now in New York said). There is the natural inclination to tell higher-ups what they appear to want to hear, and the danger that reports will be distorted as they move from level to level. Such shortcomings in the security services' information-gathering systems must also be present in the Party's.

The millions of letters to the editors, Party, and government provide the leadership with an extra channel of information, a check on the accuracy of the other channels.

Officials in Moscow put it another way: through the letters, the leadership can keep track of the general concerns of the populace. At the same time, the letters draw the authorities' attention to the short-term problems troubling citizens, which can then be remedied. These two functions, they say, add up to "a unique Soviet form of public opinion." In the West, they say, public opinion is influenced by propaganda, and is used as a tool by the ruling class to manipulate the populace. In the Soviet Union, since social antagonisms have been eliminated under Communist rule, there are no differences between the opinions held by the ordinary people and those they have selected to lead the nation. "The public opinion of the working class, the peasantry, and the intelligentsia is unified on the fundamental problems of socialist development and is expressed by the Communist Party and the other public organizations of the working people," one official said, citing the approved definition of public opinion in the *Great Soviet Encyclopedia*.

Interviews with Soviet citizens in their country and in the West show some disagreement with these views. "All the letter writing is a safety valve at best," an intellectual in a provincial city said. "It's not real public opinion, because they don't have to pay attention to it." Others, as will be detailed later, expressed fears of reprisals and skepticism that the letters ever accomplish anything. But a dissident who had moved in high Party circles conceded that the regime did seem to be making more of an effort to listen in recent years. The late Prime Minister Alexei Kosygin, he said, had a selection of letters read to him every working day. There are also signs that when a problem gets really troublesome enough, someone in the leadership signals that the writing and publishing of franker letters on that particular theme will be encouraged. This is never done openly, but careful observers of the letters columns can figure out what the approved topics are by seeing which letters are the most outspoken.

Nothing very controversial about the atrocious driving habits of Soviet citizens was printed until enough private cars were on the road to create a national danger. Then the letters began to sharpen in tone. (No national character flaw is involved here; the USSR has so many bad drivers because few can afford to own a car until middle age, when they then learn to drive.)

Other topics opened to more critical comments in recent years have been the other national menace, alcoholism, and the environmental threat to the countryside in general and to Lake Baikal, Siberia's natural wonder, in particular. Letter writers still are not permitted to cite the figures that circulate privately on the extent of the alcohol problem—some estimates say one ruble in three goes for drink—and the government continues to pollute Baikal with its pulp plant more than it officially admits. But, the dissident concludes, the weak pulse of public opinion can be discerned in these areas, as well as in campaigns for work discipline.

"It shows that they are strong enough to permit opinion to come out in the open," he said. "They are in control, and they know that they can allow something to be expressed for a time and then shut off." He gave as an example the decision to permit young Russians to commemorate the anniversary of John Lennon's murder for a few years and then to crack down and forbid the observance.

But a regime that feels itself strong enough to switch public opinion off and on is surely a long way from one that not only listens to the voice of the public but bases some of its decisions on what it hears. Allowing an occasional poll for internal use and encouraging franker letters on certain subjects is progress, but it is a great deal different from having a Soviet Gallup or Harris independently releasing poll findings every week or so on what people think about the war in Afghanistan or on the popularity of aid to Cuba, and having a regime that would react to the poll results by changing some of its policies.

Although Soviet officials criticize Western polling as part of a system of manipulation, the social scientists at Soviet institutes are well versed in Western methodology. A 1981 questionnaire prepared by the Institute on Social Research of the Soviet Academy of Sciences, for example, has a notation that 1,500 copies were printed, which means its recipients must have been the random sample size developed by Western opinion specialists.

The questionnaire is lengthy—thirty-two pages—and detailed—more than sixty questions in addition to several multiple choice sections. It starts out with an assessment of respondents' political education programs: How often do they attend political-information meetings? Do they find them of interest and use? Which lectures do they prefer: international affairs, religion and atheism, the Party's economic policy, science and technology, ideology and moral issues? Which problems interest them (and here the range is from the fighting in the Middle East to "protectionism" in government and Party, a reference to preferential treatment for those with connections)?

Where do they get their information on these and other problems? the questionnaire asks, telegraphing the expected answers a bit by listing the public lectures, political-information sessions, and agitators after both the domestic and foreign press and broadcasts, in the multiple-choice categories.

The next section asks for details on viewing and listening habits, both domestic and foreign. "Vremya" is at the top of the domestic multiple choice list. Less expected is the frankness with which the questionnaire deals with foreign broadcasts, its ready assumption that yes, the respondents listen to them, so let's find out which ones (Voice of America, BBC, Radio Liberty, Voice of Israel, Deutsche Welle, Radio Peking, and "others" are the choices, in that order). And why. Is it the music, is it to get another view of the world, to learn what others are reporting about issues in the Soviet Union? This dispassionate discussion of the foreign stations' role in Soviet public opinion is in marked contrast to the usual language of the propaganda attacks on them: centers of subversion, poisoners of minds, radio pirates. The aim of the questionnaire, of course, is to provide information, not to influence the behavior of those exposed to it.

Other questions concern problems in the respondents' workplace, such as favoritism, and their views of whether the Party is dealing correctly with them. Respondents are then classified by age, job, Party membership, and length of service. The questionnaire, and others that diplomats in Moscow say are regularly circulated, would thus seem to be a valuable tool in Party education work. Its openness would seem refreshing to a Soviet citizen unaccustomed to being addressed without a great deal of political ornamentation. Its authors' willingness to concede that foreign broadcasts are a regular part of Soviet life might elicit more open responses, particularly since the respondents are not asked their names.

It is likely that the campaign for more food and consumer goods in the stores and more efficiency at the workplace that accompanied the start of Yuri Andropov's short term of office was in part a response to polls, letters, and the other channels of information that told the leaders of the widespread public discontent. On the other hand, anyone living in the Soviet Union hardly needed special information sources to know of these conditions.

Even in the final Brezhnev years, despite the opposition of some of the old guard, Party and government were taking greater interest in the use of sociological research, above all for measuring trends in the economy. Gosplan, the state planning agency, makes frequent use of the Institute for Sociological Research, which was founded in 1968 as part of the Academy of Sciences and has a staff of about three hundred. Gosplan finds polls useful in determining the effects on society of plans to shift gears in the economy.

Although polling and other sociological research is not yet common as the sole basis for articles and books, it is referred to casually and routinely in the press as one of the sources of information on long journalistic reports on the problems of society. A story on alcoholism or crime will cite statistics about the percentage of crimes committed by people under the influence of alcohol. One story on black marketing contained quotes from some of the convicted dealers, who were from the free-wheeling Georgian republic, and who defended their actions to the sociologists as necessary to keep the economy functioning.

Another form of involving the public is to ask opinions on proposed legislation, then to pass the amended version through the Supreme Soviet or other body with changes advertised as reflecting the people's wishes. Soviet officials stress that this process is purely advisory; these national discussions, they say, are not meant to make decisions, but "are taken into consideration for the purposes of improving the legislation."

The most publicized campaign was that to provide amendments to the 1977 constitution. There were 400,000 suggestions for amendments, and, according to the official account, many of them were accepted. A Soviet television reporter said that one of the amendments accepted was his, or at least like his. He had been concerned with the environmental threat caused by nuclear power generating stations and thought that the constitution should contain an amendment stating the need for safeguards. He made the suggestion at a public meeting at his place of work, Moscow Radio and Television, and it was adopted and forwarded to the Supreme Soviet. Since there were many similar amendments from other parts of the country, he wasn't certain that his was the one actually adopted, but he rejects any suggestion that the amending process is a sham. He reiterates the argument often heard at the official level in the Soviet Union: except for a few complaints about shortages, people and government are not at odds as they are in the West.

The absence of debate even about such crucial issues as the presence of Soviet troops in Afghanistan is proof of this harmony, he maintains. Unlike the deep divisions the West experienced over Vietnam, there is understanding and support for the fighting and losses in Afghanistan because people know the sacrifice is for their own good and their own ultimate defense. The Soviet people could not be consulted before their troops were sent into Afghanistan, he said, because the military intervention had to be conducted under conditions of strict secrecy.

An émigré writer who has followed the Afghanistan situation closely said that on the contrary, opposition to the occupation and fighting there is strong, but "you would have to be crazy to write a letter to the editor about Afghanistan or any other controversial subject and sign your name to it."

Social scientists in the Soviet Union concede that ordinary citizens are sometimes reluctant to be open and honest when being asked questions by someone they identify as part of the regime, although they say this is an unreasonable attitude, since no one is punished for speaking his or her mind. To get valid results, you have to ask questions conscientiously, and often that does not happen, an official of the Institute for Sociological Research said. He considers it important to keep careful watch over the poll takers. Some of them are students and pensioners, and they may not be as careful as one would like.

When samples of opinion are needed in a hurry, the Institute uses an express survey, conducted by telephone, a remarkable advance in a nation in which all polling was suspect two decades ago. Here, again, there may be resistance to an official questioner on the other end of a telephone line. A telephone call from a stranger has different connotations in the USSR than in the West.

Soviet experts on public opinion admit that because of national traditions that go back a long way, the United States is a very public-opinion-conscious nation, and the Soviet Union is not a very advanced one in this field. An underlying current in any discussion of this sort is the authoritarian nature of Soviet society.

In a land where a monopoly of wisdom is claimed for the Party, and where the ideology proclaims that there can be no objective findings, that is easy to understand. The criticisms of the late conservative ideologist Mikhail Suslov about the "pragmatism" and "empiricism" of the sociologists and poll takers—terms he considered pejorative—have not been forgotten. On the other hand, the social science community saw in Konstantin Chernenko a champion. While still a deputy to Brezhnev, Chernenko clashed with Suslov over the value of understanding public opinion, and won.

The Party accepted Chernenko's position that without sociology and survey research, it could not determine and direct the public mood. Shortly after that, *Pravda* wrote approvingly of the work of the Central Committee of the Georgian Communist Party in opinion research.

As long as the Party maintains its control over publication of survey results, the dangers of assessing public opinion on the issues of the day seem mild indeed. But many officials do not feel comfortable about groups of intellectuals only loosely attached to the Party with the freedom to roam the country and come up with independent conclusions that may be at variance with official assessments of the situation. They contend that the nation is being well served by the channels of information that are already open, above all the letters to the editor and organs of Party and government. The advantage of the letters is that they can be acted on or ignored, inspired or discouraged, and selected in such a way as to support any position the Party wants. A regularly scheduled public opinion poll that would deliver clear-cut results for publication every month would not be as easy to dismiss or manipulate, although its questions could be controlled to steer away from subjects too controversial.

No consensus can be found among specialists inside and outside the system on the exact role the millions of letters play. Soviet sociologists agree with Western analysts that the letters are a useful safety valve and indicator of what problems are uppermost in people's thoughts. Neither group is as sure of their role in influencing or forming policy. Do the Politburo leaders order improvements in productivity and food supplies because the weight of the letters and other indicators of opinion force them to, or do they decide to do that on their own? "Probably both," a researcher now in the West said. "But they must keep up the aura of infallibility necessary to continue in power, since nobody elected them. And since no one did, they cannot admit that anyone has the right to tell them how to behave in office."

Sociologists in the Soviet Union agree that public opinion does have the potential for taking on a life of its own. If the Institute were given more power and could commission polls on subjects that might put the leadership in a bad light, as its Western counterparts can, that would be a powerful lever indeed, they say. But they see no likelihood of this happening. For the Party, the safety catch that renders public opinion polling harmless is control over publication of survey results. "They [the leadership] would be able to handle that," one Soviet scholar said.

A Western diplomat in Moscow is encouraged by the growing prominence of polls and the larger role of letters to the editor in public discussion. "But there is nothing at all like the 'turn-the-rascals-out' conditions that prevail in the West," he said. "If an American president misfires, the polls drop, and his officials scurry to adjust. The Soviets don't. The main failure of public opinion as a force in the USSR is that there is no real leverage to change *personnel* as well as policies."

But at *Trud*, editors insist that the hundreds of columns of letters they print from all parts of the nation are something real in the lives of Soviet workers, a contemporary and more responsive system of getting through the Kremlin wall than the czar's petition slot.

The letters are considered so important that a staff of 78—more than half the paper's editorial complement of 152—works in the department that investigates the problems they raise, answers individual complainants, and selects the ones that will be published. In addition to the normal flow that averages 1,600 letters a day, there are special Days of the Open Letter, conferences in which editors meet readers. "Analysis is the main task," Alexander Vassilenko, the mild-mannered head of the Reader's Letters Department, said in an interview in *Trud*'s offices, flanked by three other editors. "Through this mail, we manage to identify many urgent and pressing matters." *Trud* prints up to twenty letters a day, some of them combined in small articles on a similar theme. Yuri Mayozov, the deputy editor in chief, said there is never enough space to print all the good letters, and there are plans to devote an entire page, perhaps once a week, to accommodate more. Like most Soviet newspapers, *Trud*'s usual format is four pages, with extra pages used from time to time for the proceedings of Party or trade union congresses or important speeches. When it gets enough letters to point to an important problem, *Trud* sends its reporters out to investigate. A journalist who has been on many such assignments for other news organizations says the investigation is real and thorough, but sometimes he felt restricted by editorial control from the home office on how far he could go in seeking out officials and asking them difficult questions.

Trud's editors make no claim for using the methods of social scientists in determining which concerns of their letter writers to look into. The number of letters is one factor; the editorial staff's subjective judgment of the importance of the theme is probably the main one.

"When we get letters that the director of an enterprise didn't pay his workers on time—which, unfortunately, we still get—we might write a story about it," Mayozov said. "Another story might deal with a worker's not being given the rank he deserves. Someone who works for thirty years goes on pension and is simply forgotten by everyone, and feels insulted. These are social-public subjects. The repeating of such subjects in the letters makes us select them as themes. We stress the social importance of such subjects in our articles. The fact that we address such problems is due to the fact that our readers write us about them."

Sometimes, another editor said, a single letter will produce a story. A construction worker on the Siberian gas pipeline project wrote to complain about how poorly organized bus service from camp to site was slowing down work. *Trud* sent a correspondent to check; the worker was right, and a story was published. The last link in the chain was a letter from the worker, also published, saying that things had been straightened out.

Masses of letters come in every time there is a change, enacted
or contemplated, in the maze of legislation that governs a
worker's pay and pension. Major revisions in the pension law
brought 30,000 letters. *Trud*'s letters staff, which includes twenty-
eight attorneys specializing in labor law, spent weeks explaining
how the law, which increases pensions for those with more than
twenty years' service, affects each letter writer. The method of
dealing with such volume is to gather groups of similar questions
and problems and devote articles to answering and solving them.
But replies are also sent—it's the law, a sort of Soviet Freedom of
Information Act that says all letters must be answered. *Trud*'s
staff does not use form letters as such, Vassilenko said, but it
does have some stock language on tap for dealing with such volume. "The best standard is that the reader won't know that it's
standard," he said.

In addition to reporting back to the reader, *Trud* reports upward to its publisher, the Central Federation of Trade Unions,
whose 125 million members include everyone in the work force,
blue- and white-collar alike, except for those in the police and
military. Analyses of letters are transmitted to the central organization of the union on a regular basis. The union leaders were
kept informed on a weekly basis, for example, during the surge of
letters about the pension revisions.

Trud's editors say this dual reporting is done by the other
papers, too: *Pravda* to the Central Committee, *Izvestia* to the government, and regional and local papers to their Party and government bodies. But *Trud*, they say, is closer to the grass roots than
some of the other dailies, and they cite both the kinds of readers
and the kinds of letters they get as proof.

"Our letters are about the life of an individual in the collective,
and about his or her superiors and family life," Mayozov said.
"*Pravda* won't get letters about Ivanov's getting a free pass to the
sanitorium when Petrov didn't. We would print such a letter,
along with the supporting evidence that ten percent of war veterans in Petrov's enterprise should have had passes for a period
of sanitorium rest and only 9.8 percent got them."

Trud conducts no readership surveys as such, but knows by
letters and other means that most of its readers are workers. Sales

are high in such industrial districts as the Urals and Donbas. Until recently, there were comparatively few Moscow subscribers, but now *Trud* sells three million copies in the capital, its total circulation twenty years ago. In some areas, such as Sverdlovsk and the Donetsk oblast, people buy more copies of *Trud* than of the local papers.

Trud passed *Pravda* in circulation a few years ago to become the largest-circulating newspaper in the Soviet Union, and more recently, its editors say, passed *Asahi Shimbun* of Japan to become the largest in the world. Although *Trud*'s circulation is controlled by the government, as is every other Soviet newspaper's, there have to be some objective standards of reader interest to justify increasing the allotments of newsprint and the facilities needed for the recent annual expansions of half a million to a million readers a year. Improved technology helps; it used to take three days for *Trud* to reach the Urals. Now it's sent by wirephoto to fifty-two cities and is in the hands of readers the same day the local papers are.

Trud's average reader, as seen from Moscow, is a thirty-nine- or forty-year-old worker. But since the family also reads the paper, many teenagers and schoolchildren are among its letter writers, and so its problem solving must range far beyond the factory. The Moscow editors decline to be drawn out with questions about why these families prefer *Trud* to their local papers, although one of them conceded that *Trud* may simply be thought of as having more clout in getting things done because of its size and its sponsorship by the immense trade union bureaucracy. These are far more powerful weapons than the local Sverdlovsk paper would be able to summon. *Trud* has long had a national reputation for getting results. That was cited in a poem by Andrei Voznesensky, in which two older people, unable to get repairs for the proverbial leaky roof, asked whom to turn to. You can write anybody, the poet replies, but you'd better write *Trud*.

Trud, in the words of Mayozov, its deputy editor, has a heart, a newspaper soul. Many of its letter writers don't expect to see their words published or even answered, particularly when they concern matters of family or personal life. "But deep in its newspaper soul," he said, "it has the only public opinion we build. We are not the *prokurator*'s office, the court—to put it straight, we're not the militia. But, with things like leaky roofs, we send a letter immediately to the village to make sure it is fixed, immediately. After that, there is a follow-up, a special survey, not only to make sure the problem has been corrected, but what caused it in the first place. People in responsible positions are sort of scared of public opinion, of the public eye, when they don't do things right. That is our strength."

"A unique form of Soviet public opinion." Three million letters to the Central Committee. A category of journalism so popular with readers that it sets world circulation records. Is it possible that the voice of the people is reaching the Soviet leaders by letter rather than by ballot? Several factors must be considered in such an assessment. They include an examination of who writes the letters, their content, their prominence in the press, and, most difficult of all in a closed society, any evidence that they have brought about changes in policy or personnel.

Who writes the letters? A broad cross section of the Soviet public, according to the names and identifications that accompany them. There are experts and public figures, particularly in the national newspapers' letters columns, but there are also thousands of letters signed by the Ivanovs who work in the factories and offices. Whose letters are selected for publication, and whose rejected? Are any turned over to the authorities if the subject is too controversial or the opinions expressed considered subversive?

The experts on the topic are surely the editors of *Trud*, since the volume of their mail and the limits of a four-page paper require an editorial funnel with a very wide mouth and narrow spout. Even on a good day, eighty letters must be discarded for every one printed. But their criteria are vague and imprecise: "What interests our readers," "topicality." They resist the suggestion that themes for campaigns are handed down by the government or trade union management and that letters are selected to create the impression of reader interest in something the leadership wants discussed. In the first weeks of Yuri Andropov's fifteen months as president and Party leader, *Trud* printed many letters complaining about low productivity and supply difficulties. That was followed by Andropov's attempt to reform work habits and make more goods available. *Trud*'s editors insist their campaign was spontaneous, started weeks before, simply because the mail ran that way. Did the influence then work in the other way, with the Politburo being apprised of the letters and then deciding to act? No claims were made in this respect, either, although the editors suggested that the letters in *Trud* and other papers probably were a factor.

Trud's modest claim to be playing a role in influencing policy by gathering and making public the opinions of its millions of readers is balanced by the considerable use the leadership makes of it and other media to rally that same opinion behind decisions taken from the top. When the price of consumer goods or gasoline goes up, letters to the editor, presumably spontaneous, prepare the way by suggesting that some price adjustment might improve supplies. Others praise the decisions after they are taken. Other letters, often from groups like honest workers in a lathe department or Party veterans on a model collective farm, pour in to denounce some action of the West or to defend the Soviet Union when it shoots down a passenger plane or invades another country.

Do Soviet factory workers voluntarily sit down at their workbenches and write *Trud* about the American threat to Nicaragua? Do office workers decide, on their own, just before the government raises consumer goods prices, that it's about time to write *Izvestia* to say that prices have been unrealistically low? Officials and editors insist that they do. But some who are now in the West give a different account of the process.

A journalist who had specialized in consumer reporting had a standard list of contacts in the management of Moscow's department stores, and when his editor needed a selection of the views of ordinary workers, he would call the store supervisors. They would provide the names of one or two clerks. The managers would provide the opinions, since, as they would tell the journalist, department store clerks can't be expected to have much interest in U.S. policy in the Middle East or terrorists in Italy. The next day, the clerks could find their names in the letters column of a leading Moscow daily and proudly show them to their friends. Not only the friends but the clerks would be reading their opinions for the first time.

Another method produced the desired results with less fuss. Because most genuine letters to the editor dealt with local problems, there were occasions when it was hard to find one already on hand that provided a comment on the particular foreign or national issue the paper was stressing. The journalist remembered being at a loss for a letter about the dangers of war at a time when the paper wanted some local opinion to support a TASS statement that U.S. missile deployment plans endangered Europe. "Write one," his editor said.

These accounts show that the Soviet letters-to-the-editor system seems to be able to accommodate both genuine and counterfeit opinion, and to use both as a means of gathering information and of rallying the public behind government actions or decisions.

Those who understand the letters process from the inside are careful to draw a distinction between what is written and what is printed. The letters made public are likely to be as much propagandistic as informative, but that doesn't mean that most of the letters that arrive at editorial offices are that way.

Editors now in the West say the surveys their newspapers took showed that about ninety percent of the letters they received were about quality-of-life issues: housing, difficulties with the state economy, unresolved problems at the workplace. These are all problems that can be helped by the newspapers' pressure on the bureaucracy, once the claims are investigated. The letters departments simply forward the letters to the right offices with a little buck slip on *Trud* or *Leningradskaya Pravda* stationery, and repairs or other resolutions that might otherwise take as long as two years sometimes get accomplished in two weeks.

The other ten percent of the letters are about politics, including the ghost-written variety designed to support the government. The genuine political letters are valuable to the authorities for keeping in touch with what people are thinking, but delicate and dangerous for the letter writers. Some Soviet citizens are not hesitant about writing—and signing (since otherwise no help could be forthcoming)—letters complaining about their housing and other conditions of daily life. They are far more reluctant to express their political views openly. Only a very few of the Soviet citizens questioned for this book had ever written a letter to the editor or had known anyone who had. One, a Ukrainian dissident, was the only person who had written a political letter. That fact was one of the charges against her before her emigration. The rest were unwilling to take the risk or did not want to serve the propaganda aims of the regime, as this selection of their comments shows:

"It was senseless. Nobody writes them." "I knew I wouldn't be published if I expressed my critical views." "Writing letters makes sense only when your opinion goes along with the official line, at any level, from your factory up to the Supreme Soviet." "The editors in the Soviet Union are the Soviet government's employees, and they publish only those letters convenient to the Soviet government." "I was a dissident, but it would have been hopeless. Pretty brave and reckless I was, but with a better sense of reality than to do that." "Not only the ideas, but the words in the letter must be the same as in the newspaper." "Ninety percent of what is published is made up by the newspapers." "Someone else writes and edits all those letters." "They suppress all views that go beyond ritualistic slogans." "What we thought, we couldn't write." "Sign your name and you won't see the sky for a while."

And yet someone writes the letters. A researcher at Georgi Arbatov's Institute for U.S.A. and Canada Studies has seen the warehouse full of letters that reach the nation's television networks and remarked that it doesn't seem plausible that huge staffs would be hired to make them up. The *Trud* letter operation, including the shopping cart stuffed with handwritten mail, was genuine enough. Neither example rules out the possibility of letters being written on order from on high or being carefully screened to filter out the controversial. And there are also instances of people writing themselves into serious trouble with the authorities. A former political prisoner now in the West met a man in a camp who was sentenced to seven years for writing a letter that never got published. The fact that the letter was read by the secretary of the newspaper whose job it was to open and evaluate letters was considered proof in a provincial court that the writer was guilty of spreading anti-Soviet propaganda. Although only one person, the secretary, had read the letter, she was deemed to have been put in a position to spread the propaganda further. In all the questioning and court proceedings, one element was considered of no value: the content of the letter was true. Five men in the region had died from drinking antifreeze because no vodka was available. The letter writer was calling attention to the situation, which had not been covered in the local press, and asking the authorities to do something about the vodka supply before there were further deaths. A building worker with little sophistication, he had not realized that he could have sounded the alarm without signing his name. It was not a matter of needing to get the letter published; there was no chance of that, since the news had been kept out of the paper. The authorities would have learned of it in any case through their monitoring system in the letters department.

A man with far more political sophistication made the same mistake when his emotions and vodka interfered with his normal good judgment. He is a writer, a member of the group supporting Solzhenitsyn in his battle with the authorities. The day that Solzhenitsyn was deprived of his citizenship and expelled from the Soviet Union, the writer and his friends got drunk. As the evening wore on and he thought more and more about what his government had done to its Nobel laureate, he decided to write a defense of Solzhenitsyn that at the same time would settle some scores with the local censors. In a final flourish, he signed his name to the letter and sent it to the local branch of the writers' union.

He awoke the next day in panic and began to wait for the telephone call or knock on the door. When nothing happened that day or in the days following, his anxiety eased a bit, but he was never free from worry for another two years, when his own emigration was arranged. As he prepared to leave the country, the secretary of the writers' union felt it was safe to tell him that she had destroyed his letter as soon as she opened it.

Journalists who dealt with letters to the editors agree that trouble can result for those who speak out too frankly. One recalls working with a KGB department that monitored the letters sent his newspaper. Letters that could be interpreted as slandering the Soviet system or violating other provisions of the sweeping laws that control dissent are turned over to the KGB representative by the screeners who open the mail and distribute it. Sometimes the journalists who work in the letters department can intercede and save a letter writer from his or her foolishness. If a schoolboy writes to attack some policy, the journalist can contact his teachers and urge them to talk to him. But interventions like these carry some risk for the journalists, who have sometimes found themselves in trouble with the KGB for their attempts.

Young people, peasants who have had little contact with the authorities, and those who live in the provinces are the most likely to write letters that lead to trouble. Most other people know better.

"It's not that they don't take risks with what they say in some letters," a former letters editor said. "It's just that they don't sign their names." Or their right names. The émigré writer who had defended Solzhenitsyn has an older relative who has sent letter after letter to Soviet newspapers over the years, criticizing the leadership and taking issue with its policies. He then signs them with the name of a prominent general. "It makes him feel good to be able to get a lot of things off his chest," the writer said. A man who had screened letters at a provincial paper said the letters he saw fell into three general categories: the poem or vignette of urban or rural life, the complaint about living conditions or the myriad flaws of the state-run economy, and the hot political letter, unsigned. He considered the spontaneous letters of support for Soviet policies in Afghanistan not really to be in the category of genuine opinion.

People write poems or little stories because of the paucity of other outlets for their creative urges. Where the average American small town will have an amateur theater, a weekly paper eager for contributors, and various church and social organizations to occupy people's spare time, a Soviet town would be considered well off with a house of culture that can show fairly recent movies as a change from the Party meetings there. Men and women who live in these towns can point with pride to their published poems, on the rare occasions when they are used, or can simply have the satisfaction of having sent something to an editor.

The hallmark of the successful complaint letter is that it manages to get one arm of the government into action against another arm that had not been doing its job. "Rude bus drivers" must be disciplined, "Repair after repair" stopped, to cite some complaints from *Trud*'s letters columns. Action often does follow the letters, particularly if the complaint is general enough to set off an article. But the complaint can never go beyond the specific example to generalize about the faults of the system.

The system can be attacked, however, in the third category of letter—that composed to settle a grudge with the authorities or simply to let off steam. The writer clearly expects no response. He or she has left off signature and address, and has probably mailed the letter from a different district of the city or a different village. As the case of the bogus general shows, the anonymous letter is good for the mental health. Does it have another function, however, as a means of informing the leadership that the public pulse is throbbing a little more strongly than usual?

Opinions vary. The former letters editor is not very sanguine about the authorities' paying a great amount of attention to the letters as the true voice of the people. "The Central Committee apparatchiks and the men of lesser rank running the country in the republics and provinces already know what's going on and what's wrong," he said. "They have informers filling them in in a well-organized system, and they also have friends and relatives who lead ordinary lives and can tell them what the problems are."

An editor still in the Soviet Union, but able to speak frankly, suggested that public opinion, expressed in letters or in polling, might not have any greater effect than making the Soviet Union an easier place to rule for leaders who have some idea of what concerns their people have. That in itself, he said, constitutes a considerable step forward from the years of Stalin's dictatorship.

Getting some idea of what people are thinking is one rationale for the endless meetings that take place in work and living places and public halls in the Soviet Union. The meetings are supposed to be two-way affairs in which the Party or works officials make announcements and explain decisions and the people in the audience ask questions and let their opinions be known. Workers in well-organized enterprises can count on two meetings a week, each of about a quarter-hour. Attendance is compulsory, but since the meetings are held on the company time, absenteeism is not a problem. Soviet officials describe the meetings in much the same terms they use for the letters to Party, government, and newspapers: a way of learning the concerns of the populace, a way for the people's representatives to accept suggestions for the governance of a socialist society. The meeting system is firmly anchored in the Soviet constitution, which, according to its authors in the Party, was itself in great part originated and amended by people attending public meetings across the nation. The meeting process begins in grade school, continues through high school and college through the youth organization, the Komsomol, to which almost everyone belongs, and extends through the trade unions (with, again, almost universal membership), works organizations, and public lectures of the Znaniye society for political education.

Much is claimed for these meetings. Union members are said to come up with innovative production techniques, collective farmers to introduce better ways of growing and harvesting crops. Government, party, and enterprise officials are supposed to be able to use the meetings to solve the problems of citizens, either on the spot or by going inward or upward in the bureaucracy.

A researcher in a Moscow institute, in her first term as deputy to the city soviet, says she gets so many inquiries from her constituents that she has had to reduce her institute work schedule in order to have time enough to have meetings with them. Are the constituents asking questions about Soviet foreign policy or the relationship of military spending to social needs (issues she is highly qualified to discuss in her institute)? Those concerns, she makes clear, should be addressed to another body. Local soviets deal with local problems. They turn out to be the same ones that concern the letter writers, of course: the difficulty of daily life in a shortage economy. There is a connection between these problems and the distant decisions made in allocating the nation's resources, but the local soviet deputy does not believe it is her province to examine this connection.

Nor do the organizers of the meetings, according to those who have attended hundreds of hours of them. Foreign policy is sketched out in broad terms; domestic issues are covered along lines that closely follow the pattern of the Party press. Reading Pravda's editorial-like articles, in fact, is the way some meeting lecturers dispose of their task. As described by a former white-collar worker in a large office, the Party representative reads his clipping while some women knit and other employees eat their lunches and sneak glances at the sports pages of their own papers.

The participation of the individual enlarges as the scope and size of the meeting contracts. An engineer said that the time he spent in factory meetings was almost entirely wasted. The meetings were so lacking in spontaneity that participants actually were handed scripts. If a touring singer or actor happened to be in their provincial city, he or she would be invited to the factory meetings, handed a script, and permitted to address the employees. Often the actors would end up delivering exhortations to all to work harder and fulfill the plan, subjects not normally part of their expertise.

"I've tried to sleep at some of these meetings," another engineer, from an electrical equipment factory in the north of Russia, said. "There was absolutely nothing to be gained professionally. For that, we had our journals, including some from the West, which were devoid of propaganda but filled with information we could use."

A third engineer worked in a plant where favored workers were given scripts with suggestions for improving productivity, which would then be adopted by management. A visiting Party official would sometimes be invited, and would also be written into the script, often at the cost of higher work goals than normally would have been the case. The engineer once made a spontaneous suggestion from the floor in a smaller departmental meeting, when he thought he might be able to depart from the formal agenda of the organizers. Even though his idea was for a production shortcut that would have benefited everyone, he said, it shocked the officials, because it had not been planned and they did not know what their next step should be. They recessed the meeting and held a private conference with the engineer. He agreed to withdraw the suggestion so that the meeting could proceed. This left the way clear for the plant officials to introduce the idea as their own the next time the department personnel met.

A teacher told about a similar instance of trying to affect the decision-making process from below and getting into trouble for what her supervisor considered unauthorized spontaneity. An acquaintance, a man of mixed Austrian-Russian family, had been freed from six years in prison camps, guilty of nothing but his background. He returned to the city where he had once taught, and his former colleagues took up a collection to help him get started. But no housing was available.

At one of the regular staff meetings at the school, the teacher stood up during a period when the director had left the room and asked for signatures on a petition to the local authorities to provide housing for the former prisoner. Copies would be sent to *Pravda, Izvestia,* and the Central Committee. Seventy people signed. The following week, the teacher was called in by the director and threatened with dismissal. He had been contacted by the authorities and the newspapers and asked if he had authorized the petition. Under this pressure, he had acted immediately to stamp out such grass-roots initiative.

The petitions were never published in the newspapers or alluded to by the local authorities. But the former prisoner got his apartment. "It seemed that they didn't pay attention," the teacher said. "But they do pay attention." The lesson of the incident for her was that the authorities must always maintain control, or at least the appearance of being in control.

The most spontaneous meetings described by Soviet participants are those at the apartment or residential block level. Fewer agenda items are handed down from the top, there is much more give and take, and those chairing the meetings are more willing to listen. Part of the reason is the cooperative movement, which makes many Soviet apartment dwellers the owners of part of their building. Created as a self-help solution to the state's chronic inability or unwillingness to solve the housing problem, the co-ops now account for much of the new housing being built. And although factory workers and engineers are told that they own the means of production at their workplaces, they are likely to be more outspoken in defense of an apartment that they really consider their own. A musician from the Ukraine had saved her salary to pay for a cooperative apartment under construction while she, her husband, and her son shared a flat in a communal arrangement with another couple, as a quarter of Soviet families do. That was acceptable in the short run, but the materials shortages and slow pace of work meant that the building's completion was continually being postponed. The musician organized other co-opers at a block meeting and became their spokeswoman in dealing with the authorities. A deal was struck for a fresh influx of building supplies through the gray market (one of those waiting to move in had connections) and the project got finished.

The musician had been able to use grass-roots organization of opinion to accomplish a goal. It is interesting to compare her activity in the apartment meeting with her attitude toward the Party-organized meetings she was expected to attend. Those she considered boring and a waste of time. She was proud of her record of never having asked a question or spoken in the long discussions of music serving the building of socialism or about musicians being as important as soldiers in defending the gains of the revolution. When it came to the housing meetings, however, she felt herself a genuine participant, able to change things. She also felt that there was no risk to her or her family, because people are used to complaining about housing conditions, and the authorities are used to listening to these complaints. She was also committed and concerned in the case of getting the building finished, and not concerned at all with what musicians can do about imperialism. The final ingredient was ownership: her building, not abstract ideas, was being discussed.

Another apartment dispute involved a delicate political issue, and yet the same determination to be outspoken where property is at stake was in evidence. A librarian, wife of a dissident, had to defend her right to remain in their apartment during his long prison term. Other members of the cooperative came to her aid in the building meetings, making the point that her husband's political mistakes (which they were careful not to defend) should not deprive her of the right to the two rooms and kitchen she had paid two years' salary for. She was nevertheless certain that the authorities would turn down her appeal and surprised when they relented: "Usually, in such cases, the results are zero. If the officials don't want to give you something, they do what they want."

The results can be worse than zero when the initiator of an idea or complaint is singled out for retaliation. A translator recalls using a departmental meeting to protest the way the workload was distributed among his colleagues. Management saw the logic of the protest and worked out a system to give each translator a fair quota of the work. But within the next few weeks, the translator found himself being singled out as an office troublemaker and subjected to administrative discipline, which blocked his chances for promotion.

A bookkeeper went to a workplace meeting to express her concern for the needy in the shabby neighborhood around her factory in a provincial city. She was told that there are no needy in the Soviet Union and that if anyone needs help, the government stands ready to provide it. The meeting took no action. But her superior complained to her the next day about her lack of political understanding. She said her experience shows that neither public opinion nor philanthropy can be permitted to exist in the Soviet Union, since each, in its own way, carries with it the implication that the infallible leadership is not doing its job. If anyone in the Kremlin were listening to public opinion, she said, there would have been no possibility of Andrei Sakharov's being exiled in the Soviet city of Gorky, "since he is a true national hero, revered as much as Lenin."

Public opinion exists only in its organized form, organized by the government, and that means it cannot be genuine. That is the conclusion of many of the Soviet citizens and émigrés questioned for this book. "Public opinion carries almost no weight, has almost no influence," a linguist said in a typical response. "On the surface, there seems to be *some*, sometimes, but only if the 'public mood' about some 'social phenomenon' coincides with that of the leaders—as with [disapproval of] gays." But others differ.

If the Soviet government weren't concerned with public opinion at all, why would it devote so much energy to lying to the people? a student asked. Recalling the strikes in the Kirov works in Leningrad and the Sverdlovsk machinery plant in the late sixties, a Leningrad intellectual sees a point at which public opinion, if expressed in strong enough terms, can influence the actions of the leadership. But, he said, conditions must be bad enough, and the system of repression temporarily slack enough, to permit individual expressions of displeasure to develop into group discontent. In the two cases he cited, workers had to be appeased with wage and other concessions to keep the disturbances from spreading to other areas.

The mobilization of opinion at the workplace is clearly the main concern of the Party. With examples from every Communist-ruled country—more plentiful in places like Poland than in the socialist homeland—the leadership knows how quickly discontent can lead to discussions of grievances, how that can turn into a strike, and how that can spill into the streets in demonstrations and rioting. That is why most of the energy of the Party propagandists is concentrated on the factory or office. There are an estimated four million agitators used by the Party across the nation to drum home the lessons the leaders want stressed and to deal with criticism, however muted. In a single oblast, the Chelyabinsk, more than 350,000 public lectures are delivered each year on social and political topics, with seventeen million people in attendance (an oblast, or region, is about the size and population of an average American state). In Moscow alone, there are more than 100,000 professional Party lecturers and many more times that figure in the ranks of part-time volunteers.

It is quite possible that the Party considers this effort a defensive measure rather than an attempt to persuade. The boredom and the lack of real participation are surely no secret to the meetings' organizers. Their real interest may be in an early warning system to make sure that the cycle of grievance, discussion, strike, and riot never has a chance to get started.

An American diplomat with nearly a decade's experience in Moscow said that whatever the reason, public opinion's effect in the Soviet Union is limited to the factory and local issue level, not the national and international. Recalling the uncertainty that followed the removal of Nikita Khrushchev from power in 1964, he said that all the Soviet journalists and other ready informants for Westerners suddenly quieted down, and, when they were asked what would happen next, pointed upward. They were not invoking the will of God, as earlier generations of Russians might have, but the higher-ups in the Party. There was not the slightest feeling of participation among these rather highly placed Soviet citizens, but there was the widespread feeling that *they*, the distant top leadership, would decide, and that their only link in the process would be to be informed, with some luck, a little ahead of the rest of the populace.

"That is why public opinion just isn't a factor, nationally or internationally," the diplomat said, noting that those Westerners in Moscow during the Andropov and Chernenko transitions had experienced the same reaction. "They don't even consider the possibility of swaying decisions like those. About all they can do is at the pothole and assembly line level. Party officials really do feel responsible for keeping the system running smoothly, as sort of guides of the society, and they will respond to criticism to a point. They don't want to look bad, or to have their departments or territory look bad. But they don't accomplish anything basic, really: it's an amelioration. So, on the block, in the factories, there are ways of changing things, and the top guys at every level comply because they don't want to be blamed for making a problem worse. But it's all from above."

A former editor in a Soviet publishing house agrees with the diplomat's assessment of the impotence of public opinion in swaying the international policy decisions of the USSR, but thinks it may have more than local significance in some domestic issues and has the potential in at least one area, the war in Afghanistan, to make itself felt in foreign relations.

"Usually, people lose interest rapidly in events that cannot possibly have any bearing on their lives," she said. "And the normal international affairs of the Soviet Union are one such type of event. It's like a perpetual motion machine. People don't think it's possible to construct one. And so they pay them no attention."

But the situation changes when the Soviet leadership decides to carry out its foreign policy actions with troops, as in the case of Afghanistan, where 100,000 or more young men from Soviet families were sent to fight. This kind of foreign relations is far more real to the average person than the vague accounts Soviet readers receive of diplomatic notes and international conferences. Bodies have been coming home, families have been suffering losses, and there has been talk about it, even if almost nothing is mentioned in the press or broadcast media. It would be wrong, she continued, to interpret this quiet discussion as public opinion with the force of that generated by the Vietnam War in the United States. Even in the open American society, it took years for public concern to be mobilized to the point where the government was forced to change its course. Nothing like that appears likely in the Soviet Union in the short term. But what can be said is that there is far more interest in Afghanistan, even though it is expressed privately, than there is in a country like Cambodia, where the victims of war are not Soviet citizens.

Below the surface approval of the Soviet military efforts to defeat the Western-backed Afghan "bandits" is a current of news and rumor about the costs in lives and the family tragedies. Stories were circulating in Moscow a year or two after the start of the war about sealed coffins being returned from Afghanistan containing the remains of Soviet soldiers whose bodies had been mutilated by the rebels. They were repeated with conviction both by intellectuals and by ordinary Russians. An accumulation of such stories could be a powerful argument for a winding down of a war that has been, as far as the public is supposed to know, almost devoid of casualties or defeats.

But, the editor stressed, there is another factor in Soviet politics of equal or greater power: the tradition that Russia has known since the czars, that everything is decided on the basis of the full and unquestioned wisdom of the leader or leaders, whether or not the people immediately grasp the long-range good of what might, in the short term, seem to them a bad decision or situation. From this set of attitudes, passed on from autocrat to revolutionary to bureaucrat, stems the reluctance, if not the refusal, to listen to voices from below, despite the show of democracy in the public meetings, the letters to the editor, and the elections to the local and Supreme soviets. The issue of war and peace is the clearest example of this authoritarian attitude toward popular participation, and, as in the case of Grigory Gurevich's struggle with the media and the arts, the story of one citizen's experience is the best illustration. Sergei Batovrin, like Gurevich, is an artist, but his unsuccessful battle with the Soviet regime was fought on political grounds, the question of the peace movement.

Batovrin, with ten others, founded The Group to Establish Trust Between the USSR and the U.S.A. in his Moscow apartment in 1982. They were concerned not only with the dangers of the arms race, but also by the fact that the peace movement in the Soviet Union was entirely a government affair, and thought that private citizens establishing trust would be a good way for both nations to make progress without propaganda.

What happened instead was a furious Soviet campaign to wipe out the group and lock up its leaders. Batovrin, a soft-spoken man in his twenties who learned accentless English as the child of a Soviet diplomatic family in New York, was forcibly confined to a psychiatric ward and later expelled from the country. The group had agreed on more than one hundred steps that might be taken to improve Soviet-American relations. They included exchanging doctors and school children; naming Soviet streets after American heroes and teaching Americans about the contributions of Russian immigrants like Sikorsky and Nabokov; a joint aid program for the Third World; banning children's war games and war toys; reducing international travel and telephone costs; exchanging art and historical documents. Several of the proposals dealt with breaking Party information controls. Batovrin's group called for televised discussion programs with leaders from both sides answering called-in questions; a joint non-government commission to make regular surveys of public opinion in the two countries and publish them; and the regular exchange of television programs that would show the culture, history, and everyday life of the Soviet Union and the United States.

Within weeks, the group found its activities being described as hooliganism and its members being harassed and arrested. A So-

viet official said Batovrin's group had other, anti-Soviet purposes
in mind, not peace; in any case, there was no need for a second
movement when millions of citizens were united in the Soviet
Peace Committee, a group that claims to be a voluntary organization with no government connection.

That, says Batovrin, is nonsense: "The fact is that the official
Soviet Peace Committee is a mouthpiece of the Soviet government. Since its foundation it has not put forward a single original
suggestion but has simply toed the Party line."

From his home in Brooklyn, Batovrin has been keeping in
contact with the surviving members of the group in the Soviet
Union. The original wave of arrests, he says, did not break up the
organization. It has grown in size and strength, despite a campaign of harassment and prison terms for some members.
Batovrin lists two thousand members in nineteen groups across
the country, three of them in Moscow. Two demonstrations of a
few hundred people were quickly broken up and many arrests
made, and new tactics had to be introduced as a result.

Since that time, the groups have been staging peace exhibits in
private homes; conducting peace seminars, often with foreign visitors; doing peace research; contacting Western correspondents
when a new peace proposal is issued; and turning out peace
samizdat—self-published documents and position papers that are
copied in editions of one hundred, using ordinary photographic
equipment, and sent to other parts of the country for further du-
plication.

"We're not trying to hide ourselves," Batovrin said. "But we
must engage in forms of activity different from those of peace
groups in the West, where you can demonstrate."

· 4 ·

The Underground Telegraph

The D train creaks around a long bend in the elevated line from Manhattan, ten miles distant, and crosses Coney Island Avenue to run parallel with the ocean at Brighton Beach. If the scratched and graffiti-covered windows permit it and the day is clear, passengers can get a glimpse of the New Jersey Highlands far across the Lower Bay. Under the El tracks on Brighton Beach Avenue, signs in Cyrillic letters advertise Russian records, Siberian *pelmeni* dumplings, Russian-speaking hairdressers and druggists, and an Uzbek luncheonette where a counterman in an embroidered square skullcap sells hot *perushka* pastries.

The apartments near the El shake a little every time the train rumbles past, but Sergei and Irina[7] say they never notice it any more. Their four-room apartment is in a building so completely Russian that no word of English appears on its lobby bulletin board. But the standard Russian interior decor has begun to give way to a U.S.–USSR mixture: a digital clock and coffee maker next to the nickel-plated electric samovar brought from home.

On the kitchen table is another link with home: a small stack of letters from Leningrad in thin blue air-mail envelopes, addressed in Russian and English in accordance with the sensible Soviet system of country first, city and street in the middle, and names of the addressees last. A spiral notebook lies next to the pile of letters. This is Irina's careful log of letters sent and received, comparing date of arrival and postmark, numbering the letters sent

---

7. Who have asked that their last name not be used.

from Brooklyn and their acknowledgment from Leningrad. Three years of letters have produced two long columns in the notebook. The couple write their friends and relatives almost every week and hear from them almost as often.

Their Brighton Beach apartment is one of the thousands of terminals on the Western end of the Soviet Union's underground telegraph, an information system that competes with the official media, correcting, supplementing, and often contradicting what they have to say. Letters from the West are a basic source of information for this underground, but only one of many. Despite Soviet restrictions on direct dialing, hundreds of telephone calls are made each day between the United States and the Soviet Union. Soviet men and women listen to foreign shortwave broadcasts by the millions, and millions more can eavesdrop on the domestic radio stations of Western nations close to their borders; some Western television even seeps in. The unofficial market in audio tapes is brisk, and videocassettes are a growing illegal commodity. Soviet citizens with access to official information are often able to leak it to friends, as can those with contacts with foreigners. The increase in travel abroad means increased access to foreign opinions and news, and travelers share them when they return. Those who must remain home develop skills at reading between the lines in the official pronouncements and are glad to share their guesses and insights with friends. A few write *samizdat,* information bulletins illegally produced inside the USSR, and many read them and pass them along. A few others take the risk of bringing in *tamizdat,* material published abroad (*tam* is Russian for "there"), and make them available to a much wider audience.

The underground telegraph collects and transmits all this information, sometimes in written or taped form, but usually by word of mouth, and usually between trusted friends. Those who relay the news along the telegraph are not opposed to their government; almost all of them work for it, many in high positions. Dissidents do have a role in the telegraph system as providers of information and as particularly active distributors, but the vast majority of those who take part in it would reject that label. They built up their system because they want more of an idea of what is going on in their nation and the world than they can get from the newspapers and broadcasts of their government.

The underground telegraph—it is actually hundreds if not thousands of loosely connected local information networks, involving millions—is one of two systems competing to inform and mold the opinions of the Soviet public. The official system, organized in pyramid shape with the Party leadership on top and the millions of readers, listeners, and viewers on the bottom, is generously financed and equipped. The unofficial system is the work of individuals, with no discernible organizational plan. Although it does influence people's opinions, its aim is to inform, not to persuade or organize, as the official media seek to do. Its key members are amateurs, but they have learned some of the techniques of professional journalists for separating truth from lies and rumors from news. It arose out of individual dissatisfaction with the failure of the Party media to provide honest and relevant information, and it will stay in being as long as those deficiencies remain.

The development of the system was helped by two unconnected trends that followed the end of Stalinism in the 1950s, and a third event that came along in the 1970s. The first was the relaxation of political controls, which made it far less risky to spread information that might be considered hostile to the state. The second was the development of the transistor radio. The third was the emigration movement of Soviet Jews and other groups that established the Western terminals.

In its simplest form, the underground telegraph consists of a person with information telling a friend about it. At its most complex, it is made up of clandestine groups typing or photocopying news bulletins or making video tapes of Finnish television broadcasts picked up in Estonia.

The competition is unequal. Although the government has most of the advantages, from paper supplies to a vast security apparatus, the underground is growing in size and importance. The private information system isn't trying to put the government out of business; it simply wants it to be more open. The state, however, uses its formidable resources to try to silence or restrict the private network, paying particular attention to the producers of *samizdat*, the smugglers of *tamizdat*, and the distributors of both.

There are frequent announcements of the arrests and trials of the dissidents who contribute to the network, but new people take their places and new information reaches the broader public. Despite expensive electronic jamming and the thundering of the authorities against the Voice of America, Radio Liberty, the British Broadcasting Corporation, and West Germany's Deutsche Welle, the government has been forced to tolerate them as a fact of Soviet life. Stalin confiscated all radio sets capable of receiving foreign broadcasts at the start of World War II. Stalin's successors let their policemen look the other way as they stroll along the Baltic beaches and hear a dozen sunbathers listening openly to the BBC.

A computer specialist who used to frequent those beaches as a student in Leningrad said it was sometimes unnecessary to bring your own radio, so common were the sets tuned to London. Those were the days when everybody's favorite broadcaster was Anatoly Maximovich Goldberg, the Soviet émigré commentator for the BBC who has since died. In student cafeterias in Leningrad and in the Baltic republics, where BBC reception was particularly strong, a frequent topic of conversation would be what Anatoly Maximovich had been discussing in his commentaries. "There was no great worry as long as you knew everyone listening was a friend," another student who had gone to school in Tartu, Estonia, said. A Moscow graduate assistant said that even the KGB was relaxed about foreign broadcasts. A childhood friend who became a KGB agent used to fill him in on what was going on in the academic community at Moscow State University. The security people, he said, would routinely receive denunciations from cleaning women and porters about professors' listening to Western broadcasts. They would just as routinely ignore them, sometimes explaining to the informers that it was one of the duties of academic personnel to listen to and understand the propaganda of the other side, the better to be able to combat it in the classroom.

Foreign broadcasts are an important element of the underground information system in the Soviet Union because of their focus on major news events and their immediacy. But the underground telegraph relies fully as much on the news produced and relayed by ordinary people, without the help of professional background and technology, through word of mouth communication and letter writing.

Before 1973, when the third wave of Soviet emigration began, U.S. Postal Service officials estimate that the volume of mail between the Soviet Union and the United States was much less than a million letters a year in both directions. No exact records are available before 1979, when the two-way flow was already 2,599,000. It has increased dramatically every year since: to 3,090,000 in 1980, 7,277,000 in 1981, 10,512,000 in 1982, and 12,276,000 in 1983.

Irina and Sergei, in common with many other émigrés, say they never write anything political to their friends and relatives, but the content of their letters and the millions of others crossing between the continents adds up to a powerful political statement that is repeated again and again along the underground lines in the Soviet Union. It is that life in the West may have its problems, but is so much better by every measurement than conditions in the Soviet Union that a comparison is difficult to draw. People live well. They are free to do pretty much as they like. And their children are going to do even better.

The same message comes across even when the letter writers are too cautious to say very much about their living conditions. A package of blue jeans and a fake-fur jacket, sent by an émigré still unable to find a steady job, tells as much as a letter, and thousands of such packages are sent every month. A color photograph of a family standing in front of their new car or mowing their lawn is a powerful message, as is a picture of the kind received by a family in Kiev, of relatives standing in front of a Broadway fruit stand in New York, with neat stacks of oranges glowing against the snowy background. Oranges in winter!

Such snapshots of America supplement those already gleaned from the official media by discerning Soviet readers. Pictures in *Literaturnaya Gazeta* of soup kitchen lines show that even some Americans dependent on charity seem to be better clothed than many Russians are. One Moscow resident recalled seeing a shirt on a man in a television story about unemployment in Cleveland that would have cost fifty rubles on the black market in the USSR. Even the carefully selected books by American authors have unintended messages. Theodore Dreiser is highly regarded by Soviet literary authorities, since he showed the flaws of an American society of nearly a century ago. Some readers draw another lesson. A dissident said he began to get interested in the United States as a place where anyone could get rich after reading Dreiser's accounts of ruthless capitalists.

The letters from America, too, have unintended messages. A Brighton Beach pensioner, determined to keep away from politics in his letters to his family in a Soviet provincial city, included a chatty passage about Vanessa Williams's selection as the first black Miss America. The next letter from Russia contained a sharp admonition to stay away from lies and propaganda (it sounded as though it had been written for the censor). It took the man some time to figure out what was being disputed. Then he understood: since his relatives had been told all their lives that all black Americans lived under the worst conditions of oppression, it simply couldn't be true that one had been chosen as the most beautiful woman in the land. A government clerk who became a New York businessman worked out a simple signal before he left to let his friends know how he was faring. He would send a snapshot twice a year. If it showed him sitting down, that meant conditions were bad. Standing up meant things were good. He was always standing up in his Polaroid shots, but the background kept getting more elaborate, with color television supplanting radio, video recorder supplementing the TV, and finally, the move from Brooklyn to Long Island with a swimming pool in the picture. The story reminded older émigrés of a reverse example. After World War II, when some Americans of Armenian descent decided to try life in Soviet Armenia, they, too, arranged a snapshot code of standing up for good times and sitting down for bad. When their pictures arrived back in the United States, they were all lying on the floor.

Officials in the USSR try to counter the news the letters from America bring with frequent press campaigns about conditions in the United States in general and for the luckless Soviet émigrés in particular. In the few cases of an émigré's return, huge publicity festivals are arranged, with press interviews and TV appearances that stress the same themes.

An accountant wrote her former supervisor in a medium-sized Ukrainian city a letter that contained a frank assessment of the pluses and minuses of life in New York. For people like her and her husband, who go to night school to learn English and also study for equivalency certificates so they can make use of their Soviet education, she wrote, it was difficult but worth the struggle. They have an apartment in Queens and a car to drive on weekend trips to Long Island. For some of the older people who cluster in communities like Brighton Beach, where they don't have to learn English and can live on welfare, she added, life in America has been something of a disappointment, even if they are far better off materially than they would be if they were working for a salary in the Soviet Union. The supervisor sent the letter to the local newspaper, which printed only the negative parts of it, excluding not only the accountant's night school but the information about living well from American social assistance.

One of the tenets of Soviet propaganda is that citizens of the USSR may not measure up to Westerners in the possession of material goods (and a subtheme is that they don't, or shouldn't, want to), but they are far ahead in guaranteed employment, free medical care, and low-cost housing. No one knows better than the people in the USSR the quality of these services, but at least they have been able to console themselves with the thought that they have been spared the worse fate of coping with capitalism's uncertainty and harshness.

Now, with the letters, comes the news that it's possible to have the benefits of socialism and tape decks besides. "We heard about unemployment in America all our lives," a social worker said. "We never heard a word about unemployment *benefits*."

"At first, the Soviet people who come here want to live like capitalists and work like Communists," a teletype operator said. "But soon they learn they are expected to earn their pay, and they do." She said letters sent back to the Soviet Union discuss not only these new work habits but the benefits they bring, such as sales commissions and Christmas bonuses.

A retired teacher and her husband, who study English in free classes at the Oceanfront YMHA in Brighton Beach, say they are a little ashamed to be collecting so much from the federal and state governments without having contributed during their working careers. They wished there were some way for émigrés to do volunteer work to pay the Americans back for the combination of subsidies, payments, and food stamps that can total more than seven hundred dollars a month, even for newly arrived former Soviet citizens. But their main point was one they say they get across in their letters home—that as foreigners who can barely speak English and have no jobs, they are better housed and dressed than they had been on their white-collar salaries at home.

Not all the letters concern material goods, although lives spent in a dictatorship seem to have dulled the political interests of many émigrés. Exact voting figures are hard to determine, but Ben Lederman, the affable Brighton Beach aide to Representative Stephen Solarz, says that the number of émigrés registered to vote is low. Writing about living conditions is a more natural and safer subject for the letters to the Soviet Union. That also carries a political message about equality of opportunity as powerful as any account of participation in elections.

"I'm more careful now," a teacher said about her letters. "But when I first came to the United States, I wrote what I wanted to every time. I told them I lived in a beautiful neighborhood in Queens. I told them how proud I was to see the Star of David, for Hanukkah, along with the Christmas symbols on the television screens at holiday time, on what I thought then was the official network of the government. I wrote about people wishing me a happy Hanukkah and me wishing them a merry Christmas. I said I knew that the Soviet Union was supposed to be a multinational state, but that America is the real one. They have sixteen republics; we have all the countries in the world.

"My sister-in-law wrote back that all her neighbors and friends read those letters. They said it was like having America on color TV."

As the schoolteacher learned to tone down her exuberance, so do other émigrés. Putting the United States in too good a light can cause trouble for those receiving the letters, or so relatives in the United States believe. A couple whose modest Jersey City apartment has a stunning view of the World Trade Center in lower Manhattan (and an American flag as its main decoration) wrote a straightforward description of it to their relatives soon after they moved in, marveling mostly over the space, four times what they had in the USSR.[8] The letter logging system the couple uses shows that the letter describing the apartment never reached its destination. (They assign a number to each letter and check the number off when their relatives mention it in their replies.) The missing letter could have been stolen for its stamps, they said, or simply for its content—people on their street would be curious to read anything from abroad. But their guess is that the letter was opened, read, and filed away by the KGB.

"Of course they read our letters," the writer who had defended Solzhenitsyn said. "Particularly mine. But the volume is so great they can't read everything. And it's possible to write in such a way as to get your message past them." He has borrowed a trick from the storyteller in the *Thousand and One Nights* to help get his letters to their destinations. At the end, he writes a phrase or two to the effect that "If you think this news is interesting, wait until you hear what I have to say in my *next* letter." That, he hopes, persuades the KGB not to destroy or divert so many letters as to discourage him from continuing to write. Another technique is to write more during the summer, when many recipients in the Soviet Union are living in their dachas rather than in their regular homes and the surveillance is likely to be looser. The KGB is less vigilant then, he believes, since agents have to have vacations, too.

The writer estimates that the flow of letters has increased a thousandfold since the first émigrés began to reach the West in large numbers. The Sheepshead Bay post office is more modest in its calculations. Although no one keeps track officially, postal

---

8. Where even the low standard of one hundred square feet of living space per person has been reached in only ten cities, according to the American specialist Henry Morton.

workers say they handle twenty times the letters to and from the Soviet Union that they did ten years ago, a figure that is consistent with recent national statistics. Another factor that makes this increase in letter writing important is that the letters are being shared outside the close circles of relatives and friends. A recent émigré who works in a Jersey City office said her family burned or buried letters that arrived from the United States in the Stalin years. Now the arrival of mail from the exiles can be a neighborhood event.

An entire literature of letters from America has grown up in the Soviet Union, an émigré editor says. Every letter from abroad gets read by twenty people, who tell twenty other people about it. It would be safe to say that everyone in European Russia has somehow heard from the quarter million émigrés in the West and Israel, in his view, either directly or through the underground telegraph. In his own case, even attempts to play down his success in the United States added to the attraction. When he wrote that he had not yet been able to find work in his profession, and then included pictures of his well-dressed family standing in front of their newly acquired three-hundred-dollar used car, the effect was electric. People who wrote back from the Soviet Union had noticed every detail of his children's down coats and boots, and even praised the car he calls a clunker.

"I only write what I'm doing, what's going on in New York, particularly the plays and concerts I see and the books I read," a social worker said. "But that becomes political when it's read by my friends and family in the Soviet Union. It's very easy to compare the cultural offerings here and there without trying to make a point of it." Some of his letters don't get delivered, but there seems no logic in the pattern. Completely innocuous letters have been intercepted and some with hidden messages have gone through without trouble, including some carefully guarded thoughts about the Soviet shooting down of the Korean airliner.

One of his neighbors, a cook, said that the Soviet action against innocent airline passengers produced "a cry from the heart" from her, but that she didn't dare make even oblique mention of it in her letters. Another woman, an office worker, said there was something in the Russian language and experience that made it possible to get such thoughts across. "Americans speak and think with the same mind—it's wonderful," she said. "But Russians don't. It's easy for us to write and be understood without saying very much."

Not all news in the letters from America is accepted uncritically. Many émigrés report that the years of propaganda has made some of their relatives absolutely impervious to any revised view of life in the United States. They seem particularly susceptible to the belief that the United States is preparing a war against the Soviet Union, a thesis that many of the resources of Soviet propaganda are devoted to advancing. Letters come back from the Soviet Union from former office colleagues or neighbors with messages like "Don't think you can defeat us—look what we did to the Germans."

Those Soviet Jews beginning to practice their religion for the first time in the United States find that their enthusiastic letters on their discoveries elicit unenthusiastic replies. With little possibility of joining in the experience, the relatives still in the Soviet Union make it known they're not interested in hearing about bar mitzvahs and the celebration of the holidays.

For each of these examples, however, there are scores that show the role the letters play in informing and enlightening. Many émigrés admit that they, too, believed what they read in the Soviet press for much of their lives. Two events then led to the gradual change in this faith. When Nikita Khrushchev exposed the crimes of Stalin, ordinary people took the argument a step further and began to distrust everything the government did or said. The freer political atmosphere under Khrushchev made it possible to discuss these doubts more openly. Then came the openings to the West, of which the emigration and letters are only the latest manifestation. Before that, it had become easier, politically and technically, to listen to foreign broadcasts, and for some, to travel or have contacts with foreigners.

The broadcasts of the Voice of America, the BBC, and the other foreign shortwave stations are not considered as completely trustworthy as the letters from friends and relatives, but they do have the advantage of immediacy. It takes a letter six to eight days to reach Moscow from New York or vice versa; during periods of tension, such as that which followed the Korean airliner incident, the period doubles. The Western stations can be on the air with a wire-service bulletin about an event of concern to Soviet listeners minutes after it moves on the teleprinters. TASS receives the same Western wire services the foreign stations do, and, like them, has its own network of correspondents around the world. But if it uses the dispatch of a Western source at all on an important story, it does so only after hours and sometimes days of deliberation.

When an East-West summit collapses or a new war flares up somewhere in the world, and TASS is still deep in editorial and Party conferences on how to handle the news, millions of Soviet citizens may already have heard it from the shortwave radios in their homes. Their information also immediately enters the underground telegraph system. Friends who have been listening call friends who were not. If the event is important enough, the news is supplemented by opinions gleaned from reading between the lines of the official version. Soon afterward, the letters begin to arrive from Brighton Beach or Los Angeles and the telephone rings with an international call with code words sprinkled among the conversations about aunts and babies.

Another arrival that creates a stir in Soviet homes—although it appears far less frequently than friends' or relatives' news from the United States—is *Amerika*. No one can jam this printed Voice of America, although there have been instances of interference in its distribution.

Published in Russian by the United States Information Agency, *Amerika* is part of an agreement the Soviet Union concluded with the United States in 1956. Fifty thousand copies of *Amerika* are circulated in the USSR, in exchange for the circulation of fifty thousand copies of an official Soviet magazine, *Soviet Life*, in the United States. American diplomats in Moscow are certain they could distribute ten, twenty-five, or a hundred times that number of copies of *Amerika* if the limit were raised.

A computer specialist said *Amerika* was a shock and a delight when he first saw it in Moscow in the late 1950s. He ignored much of the text, which is a sort of down-the-middle Western objectivity rather than propaganda in the florid Soviet style. What attracted him were the pictures, the color, the handsome format on the lines of *Life* magazine. There were New England village greens, Midwest shopping malls, New York office towers, California beaches. He was certain that the Americans were only showing the best side of their country, but was enormously impressed that they had so much of a best side to show.

A woman white-collar worker from the Ukraine was similarly dazzled with her first look at *Amerika*. It was brought by an uncle who was a member of the Moscow intelligentsia, and it had already passed through many hands by the time she saw it. At least ten people in her family and among her friends read that copy, and each told another ten what he or she had read, she said. The magazine was returned to the Moscow uncle in one piece despite many requests for pages or sections, which are a frequent item on black markets. The Ukrainians found the pictures of American cities attractive, but their attention was mainly drawn to the farms.

Production figures for American agriculture were easy to compare with local ones, and the differences were devastating. The Ukrainians quickly figured out how much more per acre and per farm worker the Americans were growing, and concluded that American standards of productivity would solve their republic's grain shortages. One Ukrainian who helped keep the books for one of the big collective farms in the area noted that even the unimpressive production figures issued by agricultural officials in their region were inflated, and so the American edge was greater.

The arrival of *Amerika* in that town is a good example of how the underground telegraph works. Within hours, word had spread among friends and neighbors that the magazine was there. In the days that followed, its content was discussed and shared, and the additional pieces of information about the true state of local farm production also entered the network. The woman who had introduced the magazine was the center of that particular spontaneous network, but at other times has been at its edges.

She has never met a dissident and, until leaving the Soviet Union, had never seen a single piece of *samizdat* material. Nevertheless, she spent as much as an hour a day participating in the underground telegraph, discussing events and issues and passing information to and from friends. Some of that information concerned dissidents; Sakharov's exile and condition, she said, was a frequent topic. One friend had kept copies of the Solzhenitsyn books and stories published in *Novy Mir* before his work was banned, and that and the work of other forbidden authors was sometimes discussed. Most of the information was more mundane: where scarce goods were available; payroll juggling at the local factory at the workers' expense because funds had run out; panic at another area enterprise, a small mine, because the plan could not be fulfilled, even though the banners celebrating fulfillment had been painted.

Foreign broadcasts, she said, were mentioned routinely as information sources. Those who had heard a particular program filled in those who had not. There is more to this function than simply that of human tape recorder. Key people in the networks listen to foreign broadcasts regularly, and then analyze and interpret them. Often they cross-check the information from one station with that of another. At times of crisis, the listening increases, with the key people staying up late and scanning the shortwave dials for signals that penetrate the jamming that also increases in crisis situations.

There is usually a single person in every factory department or office who seems to know more than anyone else. He or she is the conduit for the jokes that appear, like magic, the day after an important speech or event. The jokes are so useful to the authorities as a means of letting off steam and sampling reaction that there is a suspicion that the KGB must have a joke department.

The underground telegraph certainly does. Jokes puncture official pretensions and tell the true story in a few quick words. A joke heard in Moscow is an illustration of this shorthand commentary: A Georgian comes to the capital for a one-day visit and announces that he's going to buy his wife a mink coat, go to the Bolshoi ballet, and visit Lenin's tomb. That's impossible, his friends say. Only foreigners can get Bolshoi tickets, fur coats are sold only to favored customers, and lining up to see Lenin's embalmed body is a day's task in itself. The Georgian goes to the fur store and pays double the price—one coat for me, one for you, he tells the clerk—and walks out with his prize. The same method works at the Bolshoi ticket window—one front row seat for me, one for you. At Lenin's tomb, he jumps the line, walks up to the guards, spikes hundred-ruble notes on their bayonets, and asks to see Lenin. Yes, sir, they reply. Do you want to go in, or shall we bring him out?

That joke performs a number of functions. It adds to the legend of the entrepreneurial spirit of the Georgian republic, makes fun of the shortages and the privileges granted officials and foreigners, deflates the Lenin legend a little, and shows, finally, that for money, anything can be obtained in Moscow.

"One day someone ought to erect a monument to the political joke," the dissident Vladimir Bukovsky writes in his autobiography, *To Build a Castle.* "Public opinion, banned and suppressed, finds expression in this form. Packed to the hilt with information, a Soviet joke is worth volumes of philosophical essays."

Bukovsky illustrates his point with a succinct joke that also involves Lenin's body. One day it disappears from the mausoleum on Red Square. Inside the building they find a note: "Gone to Zurich to start all over again."

The same opinion leaders who invent jokes can be counted on to analyze the hidden information in the Party press and to combine what they learn there with what is being passed along by word of mouth and broadcast on the foreign stations.

Pavel Litvinov, the dissident grandson of the former Soviet foreign minister Maxim Litvinov, spent four years in exile in a Siberian village and got to know the opinion leaders there. Everyone in the village turned to them to interpret both foreign- and Party-originated news and information, he said. When Khrushchev's death was reported by the Western shortwave stations, Litvinov hastened to tell his friends among the villagers about it. They paid little attention to his news. It was only when the man in the village they looked to for guidance told them about Khrushchev's death the following day, after a short official story had been released, that they were willing to accept the news as truth.

The villagers were puzzled by the broadcasts of the Voice of

America if they heard them directly from his radio, he said, but understood them if the village opinion leader digested them and told them what the news was. It wasn't a question of not understanding English—these were Russian-language VOA broadcasts. But in another sense, the language did interfere. A villager would enter Litvinov's home, be told that "America" was broadcasting, show momentary interest, and then stop listening after a minute or so, because the news about the Middle East, détente, Washington, or Western Europe was simply too complex for him to grasp. Few of the villagers had ever been outside their isolated district, even to the next big town, and although they understood planting and harvesting (and rejoiced over Khrushchev's death, since they blamed him for restricting their private garden plots) they did not understand the outside world. Someone who did have an elementary grasp of foreign and domestic affairs had to be added to the communication process. The former foreign minister's grandson, exiled for protesting the Soviet invasion of Czechoslovakia and other dissident activities, did not qualify, in the village view, not because he was a dissident, but because he wasn't a villager.

No such interpreter was needed for the broadcasts of Radio Peking, which condensed everything into short and simple formula messages, easy to grasp, and then repeated them. "The Soviet leaders are the new czars" was a favorite, Litvinov said, and with no jamming, it came through clearly every night to appreciative audiences of villagers. Listening to Peking broadcasts of that era didn't produce much information, but it did seem to be an antidote for the frustrations the people of the village experienced with the authorities.

The level of the Soviet newspaper for the district was similarly simple. Its tone was cruder than any paper's in Moscow, and it was crudest when attacking the West. The villagers seemed to accept a negative view of the United States without question. But when the paper covered and commented on local affairs, where they had firsthand knowledge, they were skeptical. Local journalists did little to inspire confidence. In one celebrated example, the paper ran a report that the village had been connected to the regional power grid, with all the obligatory quotations of Lenin about electricity and the building of socialism. But the villagers could still see the uncompleted towers of the line far from the edge of town.

The villagers described by another exiled dissident in a farming region east of Moscow were so alienated that neither underground nor official means of communication had much effect on them. Life in the village was so drab, and the people were so bereft of hope for change, that they simply didn't want to hear about the outside world, he said. The high point of the day was the opening of the one store in town that sold vodka and the cheaper fortified wines that are the mainstay of less affluent Soviet drinkers. Factory workers would begin to line up in front of the store at nine A.M., although because of a law designed to reduce consumption, no alcohol could be sold until eleven. By ten, some of those in line would be begging the woman in the shop to sell them something to drink, offering small bribes. Shortly after eleven, and sometimes before, the workers would head home with their bottles, and another day of work would be lost. "Suppose they would turn on the radio," the dissident said. "Would they listen to a program about Soviet successes? No more than they would to a Deutsche Welle broadcast about how West German workers all have cars and go to the Mediterranean for their holidays. That has no meaning to their lives, which will never change. They don't want to know about it—it only makes their own lot seem worse."

A man who had been a Soviet factory worker said the news from Soviet or Western sources had absolutely no interest for him. He believed it all, he said, since it couldn't possibly have any effect on his life. In the United States, working for a Brooklyn junk dealer, he keeps the same distance from the news: "I hear the price of gold on the London market every morning on my radio. What's that to me?"

A journalist who had frequently visited the provinces on assignment for Soviet magazines said many people he met had deliberately built a wall around themselves to keep out information from the outside world. They know their standard of living will remain about the same, and they don't even have an idea of what political freedom would be like. They are unlikely to be able to visit, much less move to, nearby provincial cities, and most will never see Moscow or Leningrad, even on a group tour. With their cultural life limited to an occasional propaganda-laden film or the well-worn fare of television, they may be tempted to try foreign broadcasts. Only those with an unusual amount of curiosity will listen to the news and commentary shows—these are the local members of the underground telegraph. The rest tune in for music and entertainment. Unable to improve their own lives, they don't want to hear about people who live better, or who can hope to live better, the journalist said. "It is their way of keeping peace with themselves."

There is no way to calculate the number of these information dropouts in the Soviet system, but interviews for this book show that blue-collar workers are far likelier to belong to this group than those with more education and better jobs. But, as many examples show, it would be wrong to assume that working men and women in the Soviet Union are uniformly uninterested in getting a better idea of what is going on in their country and the world.

The workplace, factory as well as office, is one of the main places of information exchange in the Soviet Union. It offers easy opportunities to talk about what is in the local or national press, or what has been discussed at the political information meetings by Party officials. The same kinds of opinion leaders who serve as commentators and evaluators for foreign broadcasts are active in interpreting what the regime communicates. Some have become specialists in reading meaning into the long and seemingly boring speeches of the leaders, which, at considerable cost of scarce newsprint, are run at length in all major newspapers. One former white-collar worker who has observed the process calls them antenna men. They are listened to, he said, because their interpretations are close to life. They use the speeches of the Politburo men or of local leaders to predict the effect on everyday life their decisions will have. If they are wrong too often, other antenna men and women will replace them. These self-taught specialists are not limited to the intelligentsia; often they are clerks or workers. When evaluating speeches, they have learned that the most important element is positioning. If economic challenge is mentioned high, they know the food lines are likely to be even longer in the weeks ahead. If a foreign policy issue is high, that's welcomed, even though it may be a dire warning of imperialist intentions, since it means the economy must be in less of a crisis state.

These shop-floor analysts seem to be tolerated by the authorities because they perform a useful function. Discussions are held openly, although the level of frankness is below that of the information exchanges of friends and relatives.

Just as some journalists have formulas for writing their stories in the official press in order to get a little news in, so do astute readers in knowing what to look for. Most of the news they want isn't on the front page of *Pravda*, which is filled with what a professor now in the United States calls "marching-to-the-future" news. *Pravda*'s back page is more interesting: sports, television listings, and an occasional feature about a Siberian bear hunter or Kalmuk poet. Short items on Party promotions and transfers are the real news, however, and careful readers can discern patterns of political change from them. The inside pages are also important. Pages four and five contain the files of the foreign correspondents from other Communist countries and the rest of the world. *Pravda* has forty-two foreign correspondents—more than *The New York Times*. The short foreign reports paint a picture of successes in Eastern Europe, Vietnam, and Cuba, and failure in the capitalist countries. But they do have the function of showing readers the agenda of the leadership, the areas of interest and concern abroad. Often it is possible to understand the reasons for concern from laconic accounts of anti-Soviet provocation in France (which means a spy scandal or defection) or a show of strong Party unity in Czechoslovakia (which means that factional fighting has broken out). Usually these short accounts are best used as an index of what to listen for on foreign radio broadcasts.

Similar formulas are used to decode the domestic reports. As one intellectual who reads *Pravda* every day noted, the first part of the story is devoted to introducing the topic, which could be something like the oil shale strip mining operations on the Baltic. The topic is usually brought up without any reference to what Westerners would call a news peg. Nothing happened today or

yesterday or even last week. That is not surprising, since, like
everything else in the Soviet Union, newspapers are produced
according to a plan, annual, quarterly, and monthly. The editors
know what most of the news will be long before it happens. For
this reason, they are able to work on two issues of daily newspapers at once, getting most of tomorrow's paper ready as the
presses roll for today's.

Nothing has had to happen very recently in the oil shale industry to merit a news story. It is enough that the industry is an
example of the success of the Soviet system, and that, in turn, is
thanks to the foresight of Lenin and the work of the current leadership. With a lead along those lines, the oil shale story is on its
way. It compares Soviet success with the shortcomings of the
West in this particular field. Although Lenin probably didn't
write anything about oil shale, a quotation of his on a related
theme can be worked in.

Readers in search of real information skim this part to determine the topic, then skip down to the section that says that,
despite all these achievements in the past, there are current problems, although they are temporary. Sometimes these problems
are related in considerable detail, and much information can be
gleaned from them. Readers learn, too, from the last part of the
formula-written article: What is to be done? If a call is issued for
tighter labor discipline, they see this as a possible sign of a national campaign, and may deduce that it would be a good idea to
show up on the job more often, whether or not they work in oil
shale. If it is suggested that consumer prices for petroleum products are not enough to cover investment needs, they know that
the prices are going up.

Soviet readers interested in international affairs have two
choices: reading the official weekly *Za Rubezhom*, which carries
excerpts from the foreign press, or getting hold of their own
newspapers from abroad. Neither is wholly satisfactory. *Za
Rubezhom* is edited with the aim of supporting Soviet foreign policy rather than presenting a broad range of international opinion
in the manner of the American *World Press Review*. Nevertheless,
Soviet citizens with an interest in a particular region or country,
including some who have served abroad in development projects,

say they are able to keep reasonably well informed on the general outlines of what is going on there. For the details, they rely on foreign broadcasts and try to get the foreign newspaper comments in the original.

Researchers in Soviet political and social institutes have restricted but regular access to foreign periodicals, and so do the friends that they pass their information along to. It is not simply a question of making a photocopy of a column from *Le Monde*, however. Both the paper and the photocopy machine are locked up. It is possible to take notes on an important article published abroad and pass them along. The safest way, a foreign policy researcher says, is to absorb the contents and pass them along by word of mouth.

Engineers and researchers in the physical sciences are more fortunate. They are able to read Western publications in their fields in both institutional and public libraries in the big cities. An architect now in New York said he regularly got the same Japanese, Western European, and American journals in the Soviet Union that he reads now. An engineer said the only barrier to keeping up on his speciality was a two-year lag in getting journals from the United States to his plant library. These sensible policies on certain kinds of information from abroad are a reversal of those followed until the fifties, when Soviet specialists were reinventing machines and processes that had long been known in the West, simply because they hadn't been able to keep up with the literature. But such good sense has its limits. It is far easier to gain access to Western publications about concrete, computers, and generators than it is to those about history, politics, and sociology.

The Helsinki agreements of 1975 were supposed to make it easier for the Soviet public to read periodicals from abroad. The Soviet Union, at Western insistence, agreed to the "freer movement of people and ideas" across Europe's boundaries. There was no rush to deliver stacks of the *International Herald Tribune* or *Der Spiegel* to Moscow's kiosks; their availability remained pretty much limited to international hotel newsstands not accessible to ordinary Soviet men and women. Communist periodicals from the West can be bought more easily. In supplying them, Moscow is living up to the letter but not the spirit of the Helsinki Final Act. They are from the West, it is true, but the tiny *People's Voice* of the Austrian Communist Party is hardly a substitute for the *Times* of London. Nevertheless, the days when Western Communist papers were carbon copies of *Pravda* are past. Information-hungry Soviet readers who know foreign languages can often learn a great deal about human rights issues, for example, from Western European Communist publications like *L'Humanité*.

The underground telegraph gains, too, from the information that the regime permits its Party propaganda specialists to impart in the official meetings. There are thousands of these every week in the various branches of the state economy and political institutions. Although there is little of the real give and take of discussion and questioning from the floor, officials are more forthright in oral presentations than they think they can afford to be in print. An electrical engineer recalls a meeting during the Israeli-Egyptian war at a time when the headlines were full of praise for the triumphant Egyptians. But at a meeting for the one-hundred-member technical staff of his plant, a Party specialist disclosed that the Egyptian army was encircled and the Israelis were on the verge of victory. That information went immediately to friends outside the plant and spread quickly along the underground telegraph.

Such political information meetings are held at different levels, depending on rank in the enterprise and political affiliation. The electrical engineer wasn't included in his plant's highest-level group since he was not a Party member. Some of his subordinates who did have Party cards were admitted to it, and from time to time permitted some of the information to leak out. The briefings for workers in the plant were fairly basic, he said, although even those were franker than what appeared in the newspapers. In a Moscow think tank attached to the Academy of Sciences, the same division of information access was practiced, according to a social scientist who worked there. Blue-collar workers with Party cards were sometimes given information as sensitive as that permitted senior non-Party experts.

Even without direct access to high sources of information, much can be learned about the Party's intentions and actions by careful study of its pronouncements, as the antenna men know. Individuals use these same techniques for their own information. A research scientist who specialized in the study of the ecological effects of power dam construction developed a side speciality of studying the press from region to region on his travels. He began to compare the official claims of plan fulfillment with what actually went on at sites he visited. He came up with a rule that he is sure works in ninety-five percent of the cases in his speciality, power dam construction, and may be working as well in other branches of building. It is that almost every time the press publishes an account of such a project being finished ahead of schedule or even on time, one should look for trouble in the surrounding towns and villages. The reason is that prison labor has probably been brought in as an emergency measure to get the project done on time. This speeds the work during the day, but causes havoc after hours, since the convicts are seldom adequately guarded.

Another signal of something wrong in the workplace, the scientist said, is the awarding of banners to an enterprise for some spectacular production record. Some of the achievements thus rewarded can only be the result of shortcuts in work safety measures, he said. One synthetic-fibers plant got a personal message of congratulations from Leonid Brezhnev. But he and others knew that the highly praised production innovations and high volume were based on a process that caused a high incidence of cancer, particularly among the women employees. He also knew of cases where good management and hard work alone earned official recognition, but said that too often worker health and safety sacrifices were the main factor.

Newspaper readers interested in foreign affairs scrutinize the list of greetings the Party sends to friendly countries on anniversaries of their national holidays or at the New Year. The sudden absence from the list of a country like Somalia is as firm evidence to careful readers as would be the story on the break in relations that the authorities didn't permit to be published. Other policy changes are announced by changes in language. When *Pravda* began calling Rhodesia "revolutionary Zimbabwe," readers who paid attention knew that Moscow had finally conceded that Rob-

ert Mugabe, whom China backed, had won the war and was
going to emerge as the nation's leader.

The men and women who keep track of the differences between fiction and reality in the press as well as those with firsthand knowledge of Soviet economic chaos could be considered
the rank-and-file journalists of the nation's informal information
network. They feed material into the system that is checked and
supplemented by other amateur journalists, who intuitively use
some of the methods of the professionals.

Comparing the local version with foreign broadcasts is one of
these basic checking steps. An example, provided by a professor
still active in the network, would be a "Vremya" item about U.S.
plans to form a military alliance with China. Countering that
would be a Voice of America news broadcast that said the United
States and China were going to cooperate in the manufacture of
military jeeps. Discussions with friends is the next step: Is the
alliance story correct, the jeep production story correct? Are they
two separate stories, or is the "Vremya" version a distortion of the
Voice's? In such a case, it might be necessary to find the contact
among friends or relatives—a reserve officer or a researcher in a
foreign policy institute—who might give an opinion. Since the
professor was in a provincial city, that wasn't possible, and
the issue was decided, as it frequently is, on the basis of believing
the foreign version in preference to the Soviet. Had the conflicting reports been about food supplies in the region, scores of experts would have been readily available to mediate.

Networks that include real journalists enjoy a particularly rich
store of information, although the process is not without risk to
those providing the material. The detailed briefings of editors at
the no-news conferences have already been described; the same
system is used, at lower levels of confidentiality, for journalists in
lower-level positions, with the same caveat: the information is not
to be made public.

Even loyal Party journalists often find it hard to keep all that
information to themselves, as Western correspondents well know.
Telling someone else about it fulfills a natural human urge to com-
municate an interesting or exciting piece of news or gossip. The

storyteller gains a reputation as someone who knows the inside details of what the regime is up to. A reputation for being in the know acts as a magnet for more information. People want to tell what they have heard to someone who is clearly well informed and can appreciate the value of their news. There is also an element of barter: your gossip for my rumor. None of this will work at all unless another element, trust, is clearly present. Only the Western correspondents with a record of keeping their sources confidential are invited back for more inside information; only the trusted colleague can be used as the link to the underground telegraph.

Journalists are carefully watched by their editors to make sure that the really damaging information they share doesn't make its way into the networks. When it does, there are investigations to trace back to the source of the leak, usually performed by the editorial personnel, but sometimes by the KGB. Punishments range from a simple reprimand in the boss's office to demotion or forced transfer to a technical publishing house. Journalists worry, too, about losing travel privileges, not so much the rare trip to the West but the chance to get around the Soviet Union and Eastern Europe.

Travel, by journalists and others, is in itself a source of good unofficial information. Government restrictions have kept foreign travel an underdeveloped endeavor in the USSR, but it is managing to increase at a modest annual rate. The Soviet Union, with five times the population of Great Britain, has about a quarter of the number of people traveling abroad every year. Most of these five million trips are made to Eastern Europe, although nearly a million short visits to Finland are included in the total. Individual travel is rare. Most people go abroad in tourist groups or as members of official delegations. Itineraries are heavy with visits to Soviet war memorials and the museums of revolutionary movements. Group leaders keep close track of the tourists, making sure they are bused back to remote hotels at the end of a day's sightseeing. On the Baltic, the Black Sea, and the Danube, Soviet tourists live aboard ships or riverboats.

Passports and visas are difficult to obtain. Trips, for both business and pleasure, are reserved as rewards for service. But even with all these obstacles and controls, Soviet citizens learn a great deal from their trips abroad. They are more capable of evaluating the propaganda about the world outside Soviet borders when they come back. They have seen some of the things the propaganda discusses, and they share this knowledge with friends who do not have the opportunity to travel.

In addition to the short-term travelers, there are hundreds of thousands of other Soviet citizens who spend years abroad. There is a permanent contingent of 22,000 military technicians abroad, most of them in Third World countries. Diplomatic and trade missions have personnel running into the thousands, as do the worldwide merchant and fishing fleets. The armed forces add about 700,000 to the ranks of those Soviet citizens with firsthand experience of what lies beyond their borders.

The occupation of Eastern Europe, now in its fifth decade, has exposed millions of young people from all parts of the Soviet Union to travel and contacts (albeit somewhat limited) with different kinds of societies. There are no Red Army troops in Bulgaria or Romania, but troop strength in Poland, Hungary, Czechoslovakia, and East Germany totals 565,000. Nearly eighty percent of the Soviet army is made up of draftees who serve two-year terms. This constant rotation, and the long history of occupation, means that a total of about ten million Soviet soldiers have served in Eastern Europe.

Americans who visit Warsaw or East Berlin are usually depressed by the visible evidence of lack of freedom and low standards of living. But to someone coming to these places from the East, the effect is the opposite. Budapest's shops and cafés have no equal in Moscow, let alone Bratsk. Soviet soldiers don't sit in these cafés very often, because the occupation authorities make every effort to keep them from mingling with the local populations, except in carefully controlled groups that meet with the societies for friendship with the Soviet Union. There is a good deal of mingling nevertheless: military families stocking up in department stores, with far better selection and fewer crowds than back home, soldiers venturing into taverns near their bases, other soldiers black-marketing jerry cans of army gasoline to local villagers. The draftees and officers do not return to the USSR as experts on Germany or Hungary, but they do bring back an independent idea of life in those countries.

The 110,000 men rotated through the tough pacification duty in Afghanistan are a special kind of information source when they return. Their counterparts in Eastern Europe are there as the sons (and the grandsons) of the victors of World War II, serving a quiet hitch in nations where no one threatens them or even pays much attention to them, except for an occasional look of icy disdain. The contingent in Afghanistan is there to fight a war in which it is hard to distinguish friend from enemy.

Whether the Afghanistan casualties are in the hundreds, as the Soviet Union maintains, or the thousands, as the Afghan rebels say, bodies have been shipped home in discouraging numbers. The cost of the occupation eventually rose to the point where the Soviet media finally had to acknowledge that something more had been going on in Afghanistan than friendly Soviet soldiers helping colorful tribesmen. A few serious reports on the dangers and the risks of service in Afghanistan began to emerge, even though they were couched in terms of Soviet advisers and Afghan patriots chasing Western-backed bandits.

Whenever the official information system makes such a change in course, it is a sign that the underground telegraph has become so active that the leadership cannot continue to ignore the topic. Rumors were proliferating to fill the vacuum left by the official media. The stories about the Soviet soldiers' bodies being returned in sealed coffins because of the mutilations performed by the Afghan rebels have already been detailed. To these were added rumors of soldiers' having refused medals bestowed for their service in Afghanistan, partly out of shame for their role in fighting in which civilians are often the victims, partly because of concern that a Vietnam reaction was setting in at home—that the public didn't really support or understand the war. It is impossible to check on the truth of either rumor. But the fact that they have been repeated is clear evidence of disquiet over the Afghanistan involvement. And they did seem to have a role in coaxing a little more forthright reporting from the papers.

Separating truth from wishful thinking, rumor, gossip, and officially planted rumor is the main task of the individual trying to become better informed. Many stories are relatively simple to check out, unlike the reports about Afghanistan. "Know your source" is the first rule. "Check it out with someone else" is the second.

If a source is a friend or colleague, there is a record of past reliability that can be checked. Those hearing the report can also decide whether the person reporting is in a position to know the information—street cleaners are not normally privy to Party secrets. Some blue-collar workers are exceptions to this rule, however, above all the drivers of official cars and the people who mix with sailors in the port cities.

After the checking of local sources, the next step is to compare the news with that reported by foreign broadcasts. Often the information on the underground telegraph is of such a limited, local nature that it would not be broadcast. Radio Liberty can usually be counted on to provide the most detailed coverage of domestic affairs, although for this reason it is also the most heavily jammed. The Soviet media are another check, with due allowance for their distortions. If these evaluation processes seem to mesh, then the report is passed along as news. If they don't, it is labeled as rumor: I think this may be true, but I can't vouch for it.

The KGB is widely believed to have its own rumor department to float information into the private networks. Participants in the networks say that both truth and lies emanate from some mysterious source in the Party or its security services. Some of these mysterious leaks are coordinated with the official news released to the media, others are unsupported by anything else in the public press or broadcasts.

Yuri Andropov's short-lived campaign to get the nation back to work made use of both these methods. There was no official announcement of the campaign, but soon men and women who had absented themselves from their jobs to shop or stand in line were having their identity cards checked by the militia. While the press, that great organizer, remained silent, the rumors spread with the speed of a MIG jet. Officials were using the underground telegraph to get the word around, according to a Moscow sociologist, because they knew it would be believed more readily than would yet another campaign in the newspapers.

At a later stage, television was brought in to reinforce the rumors. Soviet producers usually go out of their way to avoid spontaneity. Their bread and butter is the predictable, the meetings and handshakes, arrivals and departures. But suddenly footage was being shown of completely candid shots: people being stopped on the street at midday and questioned as to why they weren't at their places of work. The TV crews even joined in the questioning.

Finally, the press and television entered the campaign in their traditional way, carrying long statements on the need for work discipline and the costs of corruption in high places. TASS made public the execution of high foreign trade officials and the manager of Moscow's shiniest supermarket for bribery. Meanwhile, the rumors continued, hinting that even more important heads would roll.

How do the users of private information networks tell what is planted and what is true? In the first place, the Moscow sociologist said, they do not consider the two categories mutually exclusive. In his view, the official rumor departments are only an extension of the traditional Party information procedure of calling meetings to explain issues in terms too delicate to commit to paper or broadcast.

Some official rumors can be traced to their source easily. The person who reports it is asked where he or she heard it. If the issue is important enough, telephone calls are made to that source. Rumors can frequently be traced back to the drivers who sit at the wheels of hundreds of black Volga or Chaika cars, waiting in front of offices for their bosses. They are also widely believed to have KGB connections, since the inside of an official car is a good place to listen in on conversations. The discovery that a piece of information is officially inspired does not exclude it from the underground telegraph. It merely carries that label as it is passed along. Soviet citizens say they develop a sense for what is officially inspired as well as for the disinformation that sometimes emanates from the authorities. It is a matter of a lifetime of practice, which begins in elementary school, where members of the young Pioneers are encouraged to tattle on each other.

The sociologist says his test of officially inspired rumors is whether the story has any connection with a campaign or editorial in the Party press. Another is to determine whether the person who passed the rumor is a Party or trade-union activist. If so, it's likely that spreading that particular report was an assignment.

A scientist now in New Jersey lived in Moscow during the most celebrated recent case of rumor as communication, the Jack the Ripper incidents of 1974. A murderer was preying on women victims in the dark streets near subway stops on the outskirts of Moscow. As the toll continued to rise, the press remained silent. But two kinds of rumors immediately became available. One was a free-enterprise report circulated through the unofficial networks detailing the operating patterns of the killer. The second was an officially floated rumor, released in places like the scientist's laboratory, warning women that husbands or friends should meet them at subway stations at night because of the killer. It was only after the arrest of a suspect that the papers took notice of the case, and that was to deny that there had been any serious crimes committed in Moscow in the previous ten days, during which time the toll of murder victims had reached eleven.

The authorities used planted rumors in that case to warn the populace of the danger. A newspaper story or broadcast would have performed that function in most other societies, but in the Soviet Union, that would have meant admitting that such dangerous criminality could exist under socialism. The official rumor did make that admission, but in such a way as to leave no record of it.

The irony of the case is that the official rumors weren't necessary. The Moscow underground telegraph made use of what journalists had learned at police briefings on the killings but had been forbidden to print. The fact that a news blackout had been imposed was leaked to the telegraph by some of the editors who had been ordered to impose the blackout. The contents of confidential police reports were passed from friend to friend. During that tense period in Moscow, nobody needed an official press, or even the rumors floated by the officials. Their own sources were better.

· 5 ·

The Dissident Network

Most participants in the Soviet Union's underground telegraph are not dissidents. Most of them listen to foreign broadcasts and exchange information from this and other sources in their networks not because they are opposed to their government (although by their actions they oppose its censorship) but because they want to know more about conditions at home and abroad.

But all dissidents are participants in the telegraph. They use it to multiply the effect of the information they have gathered, often at great risk, and to further their goals of making the regime live up to its paper promises. Information is crucial to these goals. If only a few hundred dissidents know about a political show trial or the denial of religious rights to a minority group, the government is far less likely to be influenced than it would be if this news reaches thousands and perhaps millions.

The small circle of men and women who risk labor camp sentences or exile in order to gather and exchange this information act as a kind of news service—a dissident TASS—for the larger unofficial network. Soviet citizens who are not dissidents are reluctant to take such risks, just as ordinary people in the West would not wish to gather their own news from the battlefields of the Middle East. But in both cases, they are glad to listen to or read the results of those news suppliers' dangerous work.

Another main difference between the two undergrounds is the lack of a written record of the information exchanged on the underground telegraph. Friend talking to friend leaves no trace of the subject, unless they were overheard. But the history of the dissident movement is replete with stories of searches for copies of *samizdat* bulletins, seizure of notes of contributors, from which handwriting identification could be made, and tracing of type-writer key patterns. All of this is used as evidence for arrests and is quoted from later at the trials of the dissidents, whose fate has in any case been decided when they enter the courtroom.

There have been so many of these arrests and trials that Soviet officials feel safe in saying that the dissident movement no longer exists, with the exception of a dozen or so malcontents who have no standing or influence. That, say dissidents now in exile in the West, is a dozen or so more than they have been given credit or blame for having in the past, and it does little to explain how scores of new dissidents can be arrested each new year. These dissidents concede that the regime has eliminated the public aspects of the movement. There are no more demonstrations in Moscow; only occasionally does a petition demanding justice for a prisoner or a minority group circulate, and those daring to sign are few. The best-known leaders of the dissident movement of the 1960s and 1970s are in prison or in exile, and the atmosphere of relative leniency that enabled them to meet and plan strategy is no more.

Despite all these setbacks, the less public but equally important work of the dissident movement continues. New people take the place of those silenced. Without demonstrations and petitions, they seek to get uncensored information to the people to further their cause, to refute with sober facts and figures the image of a happy, democratic Soviet Union that is handed down to *Pravda* by the Party and by *Pravda* to the nation.

The dissidents say they reach as many people as *Pravda* does, even though their laboriously typed news bulletins have a circulation limited to the thousands, or, under optimum conditions, tens of thousands. They use foreign broadcasts and the larger underground network in the Soviet Union to amplify these messages. Andrei Sakharov's appeals to the West or the lonely tale of a prisoner in the Urals thus can reach millions. The dissident role is to get them to the West so that they can be broadcast back. The individual participants in the underground telegraph hear them and make sure they are repeated and discussed. The process is accelerated in times of crisis, but it also goes on routinely, day after day, with news and information items large and small. Without the dissidents, there would be no first step, no one to get the prisoner's story to the West through exile channels, no one to contact Western correspondents with Sakharov's handwritten statements from his exile in Gorky.

Soviet officials and Soviet dissidents agree that two decades of conflict have not shaken the basic relationship between the rulers and the ruled. A repressive government seems as powerful as ever. Its censored and submissive media reach every corner of a vast nation. Where the dissidents have had their effect (on this, the officials disagree) is just beneath the surface. Their movement created an independent public opinion in the Soviet Union for the first time. It has succeeded in strengthening this opinion, despite the vilification of the regime and the crackdowns of the KGB. There are even dissident opinion polls to support this claim.

Those in the movement make a distinction between dissidents and human rights activists, although both are involved in the information process. Opposition to some aspect of government policy (and often little else) is what links the two forms of dissent. Both groups reject the government's charges of subversion; it is the dissidents, not the regime, who are using the free expression guaranteed by Soviet law to call for equal treatment of persecuted individuals and groups—also guaranteed by law.

Dissidents can be nationalists, seeking more freedom or complete independence for the Ukraine, Estonia, and other Soviet republics (as provided for in the constitution); ethnic groups deprived of their home territory, like the Crimean Tatars; groups like Volga Germans and Jews seeking emigration; or members of religious communities, some seeking freedom to observe their beliefs, others to leave the country. Each of these groups is quite naturally concerned with its own goals.

The human rights movement is concerned with all. It is the conscience of the regime, a conscience that makes its stand by breaking the regime's monopoly on information. Its basic instrument is the *samizdat* bulletin, most famous of which is the *Chronicle of Current Events*. The *Chronicle*, founded in 1968, has survived arrests, raids, and numerous premature official obituaries. For one eighteen-month period in the 1970s, it did not appear at all, and the KGB campaign of informers, interrogations, harsh prison terms, and breaking down two key editors so that they would implicate others, seemed to have succeeded. But the *Chronicle* came back with a different clandestine editorial board, new people who volunteered for the risk of gathering reports on human rights violations from around the country, the drudgery of typing scores of pages with unwieldy carbons, and the danger of distributing what Soviet courts had labeled anti-Soviet propaganda and had punished with nine-year sentences of prison and exile.

The *Chronicle* covered the main news events of the human rights movement, the political trials and the invasion protests. But it also carried the stories of the individual tragedies of people caught up in the system: "Boris Zdorovets, a Baptist from the Donbas, who has spent seven years in a labor camp, has been exiled for five years to Krasnoyarsk oblast. At his place of exile the police are carrying out 'educative' work on him, demanding that he publicly renounce his religion." "On June 13, the poet Ivan Sokulsky, who is about 30 years old, was arrested in Dnepropetrovsk. He had earlier been dismissed from his job and expelled from Dnepropetrovsk University, where he was in his fifth year. After this he worked as a fireman and then a sailor on the Kiev–Kherson river steamer. It was on the steamer that he was arrested. Sokulsky is charged with circulating Ukrainian *samizdat*, and in particular with allowing his typewriter to be used by university students to type out several articles." "Ivan Svetlichny, who was working as a fireman during the last part of his term in camp 35, was deprived of invalid status after his transfer to camp 36 (because of a childhood accident, he has fingers missing on both hands) and sent to work in the workshop. Here he has to drag heavy boxes about and do other work he is not capable of. He is punished for not fulfilling the norm. Some political prisoners have demanded that Svetlichny should have his invalid status restored and be given light work."

This kind of low-key reporting, letting the terrible facts speak for themselves, was the *Chronicle*'s carefully chosen policy. Sometimes, when it strayed, readers would write in to complain, and to one complaint the *Chronicle* editors replied: "The *Chronicle* makes every effort to achieve a calm, restrained tone. Unfortunately, the materials with which the *Chronicle* is dealing evoke emotional reactions and these automatically reflect the tone of the text."

Samizdat writers were under no such restraints, as these examples show: "Can the proclaimed freedom of conscience and the right to take part in ceremonial rites proclaimed by the Soviet constitution be termed anything but a lie? And is the Soviet Union's assertion before the whole world that it is concerned about the observance of human rights anything but a lie?" (From nine prisoners denied the right to wear crosses.) "The reason there is a one-party system in the Soviet Union is because we could not afford to feed two. Indeed, it is *we* who have to pay for everything. We are destitute ourselves, yet we have to feed freeloaders. And we applaud them at meetings yet!" (Bulletin of SMOT, the underground trade union.) "After invading a quiet land, unaffected by any political struggle, the occupiers launched a fratricidal war. Our boys are perishing in far-off Afghanistan. Some die without having lived their youth, leaving behind their weeping parents, young wives, and new-born children. Who is going to count those tears?" (Lithuanian *samizdat* journal.)

The *Chronicle* spawned other *Chronicles* in the West, crisply printed and edited without fear of a knock on the door, and serving the dual functions of informing Western readers about Soviet human rights violations and acting as collection points for information to be broadcast to the USSR by shortwave radio.

The *Chronicle* was a natural and necessary consequence of the growth of the Soviet human rights movement, which began to make its presence felt at about the same time in the middle 1960s that the civil rights movement did in the United States. There were many other similarities between the two movements. Both were moral, not political, but became integral to the political process. Both were nonviolent and were met with officially sanctioned violence. Both had memberships that included those who had been deprived of their rights and intellectuals who risked their privileged positions to come to their aid. It might be instructive to those who consider the superpowers as mirror images of immorality to examine the histories of the American civil and the Soviet human rights movements.

The Soviet movement started spontaneously and slowly in the improved political atmosphere in the years after Stalin's death, when Khrushchev was groping for some way to come to terms with the past and protect the nation from such massive human rights violations in the future. Separate from these government efforts, more and more people in intellectual circles began discussing how to introduce democracy into Soviet life. They became bolder in writing their leaders, calling for a dialogue, criticizing shortcomings, and, as their American counterparts had done, calling attention to violations of the constitution. But Khrushchev wanted to deal with Stalin's legacy on his own terms. The petitioners were detained for questioning, lectured by Party propagandists, forced to admit their mistakes and criticize their ideas and initiatives. Most of them gave up, but a small number in the circle of Moscow intellectuals persisted despite the persecution.

This group, knowing it was risking further arrests, thought it necessary to turn to the West for protection. But its experience was limited by the closed Soviet society; it had no means of making contact. The story of a man who is now a computer specialist in the West illustrates the limitations of the time. As a student, he had received a copy of *Amerika* and wanted to meet a real American to talk about the wonderful place he had discovered on its pages. He called the American embassy to make contact. His first two attempts were brushed aside because the cultural affairs officer he had reached was sure he was a provocateur planted by the KGB. On the third try, he succeeded, and a street meeting was arranged. But this time, the KGB was really there. As the student approached the diplomat, plainclothes agents appeared and took him away for interrogation. They had learned of the meeting through telephone taps. The student was released, but the incident was the beginning of a series of brushes with authority that led to the labor camps and emigration.

In 1965, the arrests of Andrei Sinyavsky and Yuli Daniel for having their writing published abroad galvanized the Moscow dissidents and at the same time provided them the contacts with the West they had been searching for ways to establish. Western intellectuals immediately protested against the arrests. Soviet activists learned how to provide them with information on the case to keep the protest movement alive. The dissident loop was born. News from the Soviet underground reached the Moscow dissidents, who passed it on to Western correspondents, diplomats, or other channels to relay it to the West, where it was broadcast back to the Soviet Union by the BBC, Voice of America, or Radio Liberty. Moscow dissidents of that era can still recall what a thrill it was to hear their news broadcast by one of the Western stations for the first time. The state information monopoly was dead.

Those broadcasts led to the first human rights demonstration in Soviet history when the Sinyavsky–Daniel trial opened in December 1965. Dissidents went to Pushkin Square to demonstrate for admission of the public. People had gathered at the courtroom building on the basis of news they had heard broadcast from the West. When the KGB excluded everyone but a selected audience of agents and loyalists certain to side against the defendants, the bolder sympathizers of the writers protested, and the activist period of the human rights movement was born, with help from the West. The Western connection continued to be of importance throughout the trial. Correspondents would be briefed on testimony, and within a few hours, millions tuned to shortwave sets would have the information.

It was not long before other contributions of information began to reach the new dissident loop. As people listened to the trial news and the other early contributions of the Moscow dissidents about human rights violations, they wanted to add their own stories of bureaucratic arrogance, prison camp injustice, and forgotten episodes of history. If their news got through to the right person, they could expect to hear it broadcast or read it in one of the proliferating *samizdat* bulletins.

One man from a provincial city spent his vacations in Moscow for five years trying to reach the *Chronicle of Current Events*. He had a story of injustice to tell and the names of *Chronicle* contacts. But each time he tried, the Moscow telephone information offices, street kiosks where citizens pay a few kopecks for the service most cities provide with phone books, insisted that such people did not exist. He finally contacted the *Chronicle* though word of mouth inquiry. On another occasion, a high official in a government ministry sought out a *Chronicle* editor, Ludmilla Alexeyeva, in her government office in Moscow to leak the contents of a report on the regime's persecution of religious communities. The material had been prepared for restricted circulation within the government. The official, a believer himself, wanted the nation to know about it (one statistic was that ninety percent of the Orthodox churches had been shut down since the Bolshevik revolution). He memorized the key points of the report and dictated them to Ms. Alexeyeva while the ordinary business of her office went on around them.

Those two examples illustrate both the extraordinary power of the *Chronicle* to attract people with a story to tell, and the extraordinary precautions needed to keep it publishing. The *Chronicle* was born in a period of relative freedom for underground information; one of its purposes, in fact, was to draw together all the various currents of dissident information activity into one publication people could expect to see regularly. The movement had grown to the point where it needed a voice.

"The 'dissident movement in the Soviet Union' is not only a movement dealing with the rights of man—although they sometimes become one and the same; it is a whole conglomerate of different national and religious movements, as well as a movement for social and economic rights," Ms. Alexeyeva, who is now in the West, has written.[9] "The merging of these different forces in the Soviet Union began with the *Chronicle*. Until its appearance, the numerous national and religious movements functioned, during the whole of Soviet history, in total isolation from one another. This can be explained first of all by the lack of information among their participants."

But in a society in which uncontrolled information is considered a hazardous commodity, the dangers for those providing, compiling, and distributing it are great. The official who gave the *Chronicle* the confidential religious information knew this; he was careful not to have the actual document in his possession and

9. In her introduction to Mark Hopkins's *Russia's Underground Press* (New York: Praeger, 1983).

even made sure that the notes would be in Ms. Alexeyeva's handwriting, not his. *Chronicle* editors and typists worked in constant fear of raids. Ms. Alexeyeva once concealed more than one hundred pages of *Chronicle* number 18, three issues typed on onionskin paper, in her brassiere when she was picked up by the KGB for questioning. What the *Chronicle* staff feared most of all was a KGB raid while an issue was in preparation, because that would net them the original contributions and notes of Soviet citizens in all parts of the country who had sent in reports and who could be tracked down.

To protect its contributors, the *Chronicle* devised and made public a system that probably has its roots in anti-czarist underground groups. "Anyone who is interested in seeing that the Soviet public is informed may easily pass on information to the *Chronicle*," a note in issue number 5, at the end of the first year of publication, said. "Simply tell it to the person from whom you received the *Chronicle*, and he will tell the person from whom he received the *Chronicle*, and so on. But do not try to trace back the whole chain of communication yourself, or else you will be taken for a police informer."

Ms. Alexeyeva, a cheerful woman in her mid-fifties who has survived KGB raids and interrogation not only on the *Chronicle* but on the Helsinki Watch committee in Moscow she helped found, said that the *Chronicle* both baffled the authorities and protected itself by its lack of central organization. The KGB kept looking for the center, the "single person they insisted must have been directing the operations of the *Chronicle*," she said. Such an assumption is logical in the hierarchical world of the Soviet government, but no such center or single person existed. The *Chronicle* had been founded by eight dissidents at an informal meeting in someone's apartment, and in the nearly two decades of its existence, has been produced—also in someone's apartment—by a loosely rotating system of volunteer help. The criteria for editing the *Chronicle* have not been journalistic credentials (although many have had them) but availability and willingness to risk prison or to undertake long evenings of work concealed in a back room of an apartment considered safe from the police.

Ms. Alexeyeva, during one of her frequent interrogations by

the KGB, was once asked repeatedly about the "central office" of the *Chronicle*. She was promised leniency for a friend the KGB had arrested in its crackdown on the operation. She could not comply, even if she had wanted to, she said, because there was no headquarters, no center. The KGB agents, who had never experienced a genuinely broad-based movement in Soviet political life, remained baffled but unconvinced.

Such KGB harassment culminated in the early 1970s with a concerted drive against the *Chronicle*, which dissidents say bore the KGB designation of Case 24. It was this drive that put the *Chronicle* out of business for a year and a half, turned friend against friend in the dissident movement, forced labor camp survivors like Pytor Yakir and Viktor Krasin to disavow their *Chronicle* connections and inform on their colleagues for fear of new sentences, and ended the public phase of the dissident movement. The *Chronicle* returned, publishing at greater intervals but with increased amounts of material. But the information system was crippled. Ordinary citizens did not want to be associated with dissidents now that the dangers had been made so clear in the series of show trials Case 24 produced.

For those already in the movement, it was no longer possible to hold open meetings to exchange news in the apartments of the Moscow intellectuals. Of the six known founders of the *Chronicle*, two, Krasin and Yakir, had recanted; three, Natalia Gorbanevskaya, Gen. Petr Grigorenko, and Pavel Litvinov were exiled to the West, after sentences in psychiatric wards for the first two and in Siberia for Litvinov; and one, Ilya Gabai, had committed suicide.

The dissident information network still existed, but it had to be broken down into a series of separate circles. The links that had grown among the writers fighting censorship in Moscow, the nationalists defying Russification in the Georgian Republic, and the Catholics protesting church closings in Lithuania did not break entirely, because the *Chronicle* brought their information and accusations together on its pages, but they did become less close.

When the Soviet Union signed the Helsinki agreements in 1975, trading Western acceptance of the division of Europe for soon-to-be-broken promises to observe human rights, the dissident movement had a brief public resurgence. Western diplomacy forced the Soviet negotiators to agree to the principle that the observation of human rights and the preservation of peace are inseparable, and that, viewed in this light, the violation of those rights cannot be considered purely a domestic affair. Soviet dissidents, with Ludmilla Alexeyeva in the forefront, formed monitoring groups to hold the regime to its promises. But it was not long before the Helsinki Watch committees were broken up and their members imprisoned or exiled, thus adding to the human rights violations they were supposed to be preventing.

But the Helsinki process had a longer term effect on the dissident movement and its role in supplying uncensored information to the Soviet people. It committed Western governments to paying official attention to Soviet domestic behavior, something that previously had been limited to Western intellectuals acting as individuals. The West's channel of information was mainly the battered survivors of the human rights movement, who, despite an unceasing campaign of arrests, imprisonment, and exile, managed to provide most of the material used by the West in calling attention to rights violations at the Madrid conference reviewing Helsinki compliance.

This new Western commitment also showed that outside pressure can achieve results inside the Soviet system. With camps filled with political prisoners, two Nobel prize winners in exile for their human rights activities, and hundreds of the Soviet Union's most courageous spirits and best minds silenced or in emigration, Moscow could be thought to be ignoring this pressure fairly successfully. The authorities do make a good case for their defiance of world public opinion. But they also show by some of their actions that they pay attention to it.

The most conspicuous result of Western pressure is the practice of exiling, rather than imprisoning, many human rights advocates, authors who publish abroad, and religious and nationalist activists. The worldwide protest over the first writers' trial, that of Sinyavsky and Daniel, apparently convinced the authorities that expulsion or deprivation of citizenship while abroad achieved the same end with less trouble.

What they failed to take into account was the proliferation of *tamizdat*, and the role the works would play in the internal information networks.

"This is a new opportunity for freedom of speech in our country," Ludmilla Alexeyeva said. "Our independent literature has been enriched by many new names and many new themes." Forced to emigrate in 1977 for her work on the *Chronicle* and the Helsinki Watch Group, she continues her activist role in the United States, serving as part of the broadcast link between the dissidents and the larger circles of Soviet people seeking independent information. In a country cottage in the New York suburbs crowded with books, *samizdat* manuscripts, and periodicals, she works on articles and broadcast scripts and keeps in constant touch with the surviving members of the movement in the USSR. The cottage is sparsely decorated with wooden plates and other objects of Russian country design. It could be a dacha in Peredelkino, the writers' colony in the Moscow suburbs, except for the carelessness with which the *samizdat* material is displayed.

Ms. Alexeyeva is a part of the large and lively body of émigrés in close contact with the society they were forced to leave, a phenomenon that hasn't existed since the nineteenth-century czars used similar methods against their dissident intellectuals. Unlike the previous émigré groups that left the country during the civil war of the 1920s or after World War II, these men and women are able to write and comment on current events in terms that are not divorced from reality by time and differences in outlook. Their upbringing has been Soviet; their idiom is Soviet. They are constantly refreshed by the visitors and publications that make their way westward across the borders of the Soviet Union, and they contribute, in turn, to the flow of writing and broadcasting heading eastward, back into the country.

The result is that people in the Soviet Union with no connection whatever to dissidents or exiled writers nevertheless have access to underground literature as well as information on current events. This access is not confined to the intellectuals, as conversations with Soviet citizens and émigrés show, although the intellectuals are more active in seeking it out than are ordinary people. A visit to the Moscow journalists' club or an evening with Soviet academics reveals a thorough knowledge of what is going on in the West among the Soviet citizens present, with particular attention paid to the triumphs and defeats of the Soviet émigrés, not necessarily in that order. An informal poll taken of recent arrivals in the United States, a dozen men and women enrolled in an English class in Brighton Beach, mostly working class with a few white-collar workers and teachers, showed a ready knowledge of *samizdat* and *tamizdat*. One woman could recite a long poem by a banned woman poet whose name she had forgotten. Another told of having read a copy of Bulgakov's *The Master and Margarita*, the satirical novel of the 1930s, which at that time had been banned. A third had been able to get a *samizdat* copy of *Letters to a Friend*, the memoirs Svetlana Alluyeva wrote after her defection to the West. Not all underground literature is of high quality. A dissident exiled in Siberia said the level in his village was gossip about cosmonauts' wives. But both Bulgakov and gossip provide a better picture of reality than the touched-up pictures painted by the Party press.

The physical contrast is also striking. Soviet newspapers don't have full-color weather maps or front-page pictures and graphs designed to lure readers away from their color televisions, as is the case in the United States. But they are professionally laid out, composed, and printed, and there are even a few spots of blue and red to liven the pages of weekend editions of *Literaturnaya Gazeta*. They are also available in the multiple millions for a giveaway price of the equivalent of six cents a copy, reasonable even for poorly paid Soviet wage earners, and if that is too much, they can be read in showcases along main streets and in city parks.

Most *samizdat* publications are blurry carbon copies on crackly onionskin paper, devoid of pictures, color, and even margins in most cases so as to make the best use of scarce materials. The language is direct and simple, a deliberate departure from the pomposity of *Pravda* and its sister papers. Facts, figures, dates, and details fill these bulletins, another studied departure from the official press's emphasis on exhortation, empty rhetoric, and vague phrases. These frail bulletins, in fact, look exactly like *Pravda*'s predecessors, the typewritten underground sheets edited by Lenin when the Party was illegal, and now proudly displayed in museums and collections of newspaper history.

The dissident network and shortwave broadcasts make it possible, however, for the *samizdat* news to reach an audience many times larger than Lenin's bulletins could. In some ways, the crackdown on dissident activity has hindered distribution of the actual typed bulletins, but in other ways it has helped. Dissidents dismissed from their jobs or back from prison terms and exile often go to work in factories or on construction projects, since they are considered too unreliable to return to their former posts in offices or institutes. But that gives them direct contact with blue-collar workers, a group that is usually not well represented in human rights activist circles (although often, because of religion or nationality, active in other dissident concerns). Another direct link is an underground labor group, which leaves to others the *samizdat* news about political prisoners and minority persecutions and concentrates on the practical, day-to-day concerns of workers. Its *samizdat* publications have area-by-area listings of where meat and consumer goods are available, not only in the stores but in the special reserves of large enterprises. There is information on housing construction, waiting lists, and eligibility, and warnings about unsafe or harsh conditions in factories and mines.

This and other dissident information can reach the broader underground telegraph directly—this happens when a nondissident receives or is told about *samizdat* material and then tells a friend about it. A more effective way for the activists to reach the wider audience, however, is through the loop that starts in the USSR with preparation of a *samizdat* report and is completed when that report is broadcast, listened to, and passed along from friend to friend.

All elements of the loop are important, but none more so than the dissidents in the Soviet Union and the émigrés in the West who get the material out of the country and send it back on shortwave. Someone, usually in Moscow or another large city, must serve as a collection and distribution center, with all the risks that that entails. Not all the material that comes in is of front-page or newscast quality. Uneducated workers sometimes contribute rambling discourses that nevertheless contain a core of important information. Exiles send in poems or descriptions of their surroundings. Some of the writing is of interest only to the writer, but the dissidents who pass it along say it is important nevertheless as a means of expression in a society where it is almost impossible for individuals to express themselves. "These are ordinary people with a story to tell, and sometimes they tell it in improper language, with misspellings," Ms. Alexeyeva said. "Not all *samizdat* writing is done by intellectuals."

How the material in circulation in the Soviet underground gets to the West is something that those concerned do not want to discuss in detail. The diplomatic pouches of Western embassies are believed to be a main means, but it is impossible to obtain official confirmation of this. American diplomats say the Carter administration discouraged this practice as relations with the Soviet Union began to worsen, but that it probably has been restored.

One person instrumental in the loop operation confided that blue jeans from the West are one way of compensating those who run up postage and telephone bills in the Soviet Union. A way of spreading the risk is to use large numbers of people. The KGB's resources, although considerable, are not up to the task of twenty-four-hour surveillance of a student who might receive a *samizdat* news bulletin once every two months. Nevertheless, the stakes are high: seven years in a labor camp, followed by the possibility of four more in exile, for those convicted of disseminating anti-Soviet propaganda. And although the dissidents insist their work is neither illegal nor anti-Soviet, and point to a very low incidence of incorrect reports in the *Chronicle*, when they are arrested with the evidence they are almost certain of conviction by the courts. But there are always others ready to step forward to take their place, in full knowledge of the risks.

Telephoning contacts in the West with dissident information is fairly safe, since international telephone traffic has grown to the point where it cannot be satisfactorily monitored by the KGB. In the Soviet Union, a caller can use a public booth at a post office, and would not normally be asked for identification. Calls must be placed to a number not listed on any KGB compilation of the exiled activists, but it is easy to arrange the use of a neutral number in a borrowed apartment or office in Paris or New York.

Calls made from the American side cannot be traced by Soviet authorities to an individual number in the United States. They are reported to the Soviet operators only as "New York calling," not by name or number, and the émigrés feel free to call from home, often to a prearranged neutral number in a Soviet city.

Most conversations would be of little surface interest to any KGB operative listening in. The calling parties don't use their last names and refer to others only by first or code name. "How is Kolya?" "He's out of Moscow right now, with Vera. She hasn't been feeling well." Both sides know that the first person has joined the second in a labor camp, and that the second is on a hunger strike. In a short time, listeners in the Soviet Union know it, too.

It is hard for Westerners to understand why anyone would take such risks to gain access to or to pass along forbidden information. They have had a surfeit of information all their lives. Americans throw away more information from their daily quota of junk mail than Soviet citizens get from a week of watching television or reading the official press, Ms. Alexeyeva noted. "But there is a basic human need for information," she continued, "and the Soviet people are just like every other people—they want it. Their government starves them because of its fear of losing control over them. But this means they develop sharper senses for information gathering than Westerners have. To survive, you have to learn. And so they can arrest and rearrest our activists, but they cannot quiet them, and they cannot quiet the people's hunger for information."

The KGB offensive against the dissidents did not completely silence the movement, but it deprived it of its best leaders, broke the links between the human rights group and the religious and nationalist dissidents, and demoralized many people on the fringes of the movement who thought their access to independent information would end.

The movement responded by limiting itself to the most essential activities and conducting them clandestinely. It continued to help members who had lost their jobs, to collect money for families of prisoners, and, above all, to gather and disseminate information. Only a few people—thirty at the most—take public roles. The rest operate in what the dissidents call "the invisible region." The small group of activists, necessary in order to be able to contact Western correspondents, is repeatedly hit with arrests, apartment searches, and job dismissals. When one of its members must be replaced, a volunteer appears from the invisible region. The modest size of this public effort, in contrast to the expansiveness of the past, leads to the impression that the dissident movement is faltering or has been choked off. Dissidents point to the premature reports of the death of the movement made in 1968, 1973, 1977, and many times since 1980. But they do concede that the links among its various groups have been greatly weakened, which in turn weakens its ability to provide a broader spectrum of information.

One lasting result of the activism that began in the sixties is a strengthening of the underground information networks that are not limited to dissident material. Although some form of *samizdat* news has been circulating since the founding of the Soviet state (and under the czars as well), the dissidents have made it easier to obtain and socially, if not legally, acceptable.

In the years when it could operate in relative freedom, the dissident movement had the effect of loosening up the information process in society as a whole. It widened the circles of friends in the intellectual communities that provide so much information to the underground telegraph.

Evidence of the continued activity and influence of the underground information systems was supplied by two polls taken by dissident sociologists, and, of course, conducted clandestinely. The first, in 1980, questioned people in Moscow and its suburbs and some other large cities about their attitude toward Andrei Sakharov. The second, a year later, asked the same kind of audience what it thought about the Solidarity movement in Poland. The results of both polls were about the same: sixty percent of those polled said they couldn't answer because they didn't have sufficient information. The forty percent who did answer were divided about equally between supporters and critics of Sakharov, and the same division applied to Solidarity.

In a Western context, these results would have been interpreted as showing that the respondents were both unusually ill-informed and hostile to Sakharov and Solidarity. Public figures and movements that get only a twenty-percent approval rating are not considered very important.

In a Soviet context, the results were considered nothing less than sensational. They were seen as evidence that the private information networks have made considerable inroads against the official silence or vilification used to deal with Sakharov's human rights appeals and the Polish movement's pressures for democracy. Two of every five persons questioned knew about the two controversies; one of every five dissented from the official line. The Sakharov results were seen by human rights activists as particularly encouraging for the movement as well as the man, since they showed the human rights message was reaching a good part of the population and was favorably received by half that group.

Dissidents concede, however, that both the impact and the size of their movement are difficult to measure. Ms. Alexeyeva has counted the names of human rights advocates who either signed documents and petitions or were mentioned in the *Chronicle.* Her figure is about 3,300—"not very large," as she notes. But, using equally careful and conservative methods, she has also calculated much larger memberships in the single-issue dissident groups: 290,000 for religious dissenters, including 148,000 Catholics, and 187,000 for nationalist movements, including 130,000 Crimean Tatars deprived of their homelands in World War II because some of them collaborated with the Germans. The total is close to half a million.

"The public role of the human rights movement thus far exceeds its numbers," she says, "since it is the human rights movement's ideology that has turned out to be, under Soviet conditions, the only ideology capable of uniting the nationalist and religious movements that are far greater in number." This, she says, signifies not only increased opportunities for democratic ideas to reach the non-Russian populations of the USSR, but the beginnings of political pluralism: "Although few in number, dissidents in our special society perform those functions which in a normal society belong to the press and parliamentary opposition.

Only dissidents have overcome the state monopoly on information, and dissidents constitute the only moral and intellectual opposition." To those who might think that such a claim is arrogant, since no one has elected the dissidents to any office, she notes that no one has ever really been elected to the Supreme Soviet, either.

No one in the movement underestimates the determination of the regime to restore its monopoly on information or the resources at its disposal to make the attempt. A thicket of laws is designed to make almost every kind of clandestine printing or reproduction subject to severe punishments. No individual is permitted to employ labor (a law frequently skirted by high officials who have servants). If anyone should decide to do all the work without help, there is another law that specifically bans operating any reproductive apparatus, from photocopier to rotary press, unless the operator is the state.

More serious is a law that makes it possible for the authorities to extend labor camp sentences by as much as five years for those prisoners already serving terms who are considered dangerous or unrepentant. That raises the penalty for circulating *samizdat* to a possible twelve years in the camps. It also seems intended to stop or slow the circulation of *samizdat* material from the camps—one of the richest sources—to the world outside. It is easy to see how judges could find this behavior both dangerous and unrepentant.

Dissidents in the West say that the KGB has refined its techniques for identifying the typefaces on typewriters used to reproduce *samizdat* bulletins. There is supposed to be a strict registration system, akin to gun control, that would enable the police to track a type sample to the owner of the typewriter. But the system breaks down in the maze of the Soviet black market, where typewriters change hands many times and the chain of owners gets blurred or broken.

The Soviet Union's dissident information network in the 1980s thus must contend with the same shifting combination of dangers and opportunities that has been its experience since its founding. Even the crackdowns present new proof of the vitality of the movement and its permanent and growing place in Soviet life. Reports from the provinces about trials of *samizdat* writers and distributors can be viewed as proof of the KGB's wide nets and vigilance. But they also suggest that intellectuals in places like the Siberian city of Tomsk, an old university town, are no more satisfied than those in Moscow with what they are fed by the Party press.

From its founding in 1968 until 1972, the *Chronicle of Current Events* reported news from thirty-five different places. By 1981, 142 different places were mentioned in a single issue.

The KGB claims of complete success in eliminating the dissident and human rights movements are viewed with some skepticism by a population that is used to hearing inflated official statements about overfulfilled work quotas and the successes of the five-year plans.

The claims are flatly contradicted every time a new issue of the *Chronicle* appears, or the faint carbon of a labor camp news bulletin reaches prisoners' families on the outside, or the Western shortwave stations broadcast this and other news and information to listeners across the Soviet Union.

• 6 •

The Voices of America

Since the end of World War II, the United States has been broadcasting to the Soviet Union with a variety of aims and policies that change with new administrations and the state of U.S.–Soviet relations. The first Voice of America English-language broadcasts, in 1942, praised Stalin and the Soviet people for their fight against the Germans. In later years, there were calls to roll back Communism, then to contain it; attempts to liberate the Soviet population, then to enlighten it, and finally, simply to inform it.

A chart of the policy line would show many more valleys than peaks. Only the wartime alliance, some of the Kennedy–Khrushchev years, and the detente of the 1970s could be considered periods when the general tone of American broadcasts to the USSR was positive or at least neutral. In between, and since, is a plethora of low points, beginning in 1947, when the VOA first started broadcasting in Russian as the Truman administration's answer to the Moscow Radio attacks that accompanied the breakup of the alliance. Others include 1952, when Radio Liberty, at that time briefly called Radio Liberation, was set up with secret Central Intelligence Agency funding; the McCarthy period, when investigations frightened government broadcasters into taking an even harder anti-Soviet line; the reactions to Soviet invasions or interventions in Hungary, Czechoslovakia, Afghanistan, and Poland; and finally the Carter Administration's introduction of sharp-edged "commentaries," mostly on Soviet human rights abuses, and the stridently anti-Soviet "editorials" of the Reagan administration.

For all the policy changes, the American broadcasts are so superior to the local Soviet product in honesty, fairness, completeness, and candor, that they have continued to attract a large audience in the USSR. As audience research conducted for the stations and the interviews for this book show, people listen for many different reasons. Some simply want to learn about the United States and other foreign countries without having the information filtered by their own media. Others have special interests like science, and find it more openly discussed on the foreign programs, or jazz and popular music, and find it more frequently played. All are interested in a source of information and news that they may not always believe but that will always be available as a check on the generally accepted unreliability of their own broadcasts and newspapers.

Few of these listeners can know or care very much about the three elements in the United States that shape broadcast policy: the shifts in line toward the Soviet Union by successive administrations, the domestic political considerations, and the infighting among management and staffs of the stations. But these three factors mean that the United States' broadcasting to the Soviet Union is a heavily politicized affair at all times, and that sometimes the broadcasts are less effective than they could be.

Politics enters the broadcasting field so insistently because the goal of influencing Soviet behavior is so enticing. So is the companion goal (perhaps more attainable) of projecting an idea of the American way of life to the rest of the world. The politicization of broadcasting and the resultant swings in tactics are probably inevitable as long as sending out shortwave messages to other continents remains such an unpredictable enterprise.

Send airplane salespeople abroad and soon foreign airlines are flying Boeings. Send agricultural experts and green revolutions take place. There are no such immediate returns for the money spent on broadcasting. Columbia's former journalism dean, Edward W. Barrett, who had dealt with the VOA as a State Department official, wrote that "no one could prove last year's funds had been well-spent by producing a cage filled with 7,000 Russians who had deserted Communism."[10]

Others involved with the American stations for decades sometimes find it difficult to describe their effect on the audiences targeted. They agree that the Soviet public now knows more about the United States and its policies because of the Voice, and that, because of the attention Radio Liberty pays to domestic themes, the Soviet media are marginally more accurate and informative than they were in the Cold War days.

Those are no small achievements for activities as imprecise and uncertain as broadcasting and propaganda. But some of the critics in Washington and the exile centers of Munich and Paris think that the time, money, and effort devoted to the stations ought to be bringing better returns.

With two radio stations and many factions among the critics, some basic explanations are in order. The Voice of America, which began in 1942 as a part of the Office of War Information, now functions under OWI's peacetime successor, the United States Information Agency, with a three-point charter passed as law by Congress. Point one calls on it to be a consistently reliable and authoritative source of news and to broadcast news that is accurate, objective, and comprehensible. The Voice "will represent America, not any single segment of American society," point two says. In the final point, the station is mandated to "present the policies of the United States clearly and effectively [and] also present responsible discussion and opinion on these policies."

Radio Liberty became an open voice, supported by the government, after journalists exposed the CIA connection and Congress created the Board for International Broadcasting as a funding and supervisory agency. Radio Liberty differs from the Voice in mission and focus. Its audience is the Soviet Union, not the world. The VOA broadcasts in forty-two languages, including English; RL broadcasts in Russian and fourteen other languages spoken in the

---

10. As quoted in Donald R. Browne's *International Radio Broadcasting* (New York: Praeger, 1982).

Soviet Union, but not in English. It also provides more detailed coverage of events in the Soviet Union than does the Voice.

"In contrast to the Voice of America, whose primary mission is to present U.S. policy and to project U.S. society and institutions, RFE (which broadcasts to Eastern Europe) and RL seek to identify with the interests of their listeners, devoting particular attention to developments in and directly affecting the peoples of Eastern Europe and the USSR," the stations' program policy guidelines say. "In focusing on the special concerns of their audiences, they perform some of the functions of a 'home service' as well as a surrogate free press."

It is not as easy to classify the critics. The simple label of hard- or soft-liner does not fit many of them. There are the differences one would expect between those advocating a tougher anti-Soviet tone in the broadcasts and those who want politics kept more in the background. But some hard-liners think Radio Liberty is justified in broadcasting anti-Communist statements of such an intensity that democratic institutions are attacked for their weakness in the process. Others in the same general faction oppose this tendency energetically. Some of those advocating a quieter line toward the USSR think VOA editorials are acceptable, but question the quality and tone of those produced by the Reagan appointees. Another group insists that the Voice's reputation for broadcasting objective news is compromised by any editorializing, no matter how carefully labeled. Adding to the complexity of the situation is the variety of sources of criticism. The ranks of the critics include staff members of both stations, administration officials, and legislators and staff aides from both houses of Congress.

It is not hard to find Democrats and liberal Republicans convinced that the effectiveness of the VOA is being hampered by the ideological changes that were swept in with the Reagan administration in 1980. They question the content and stridency of the broadcasts and wonder whether the charter they approved in 1976 provided for a Voice of America that reflects the personal views of the president.

The best way to examine the issue is to look at what is being broadcast. A week's news broadcasts in the English language service were made available by the VOA, along with a month's run of the editorials, thirty in all. The dates were chosen at random. These main impressions emerged: The editorials were tough, argumentative, and overwhelmingly concerned with the Soviet Union; their tone, however, was not reflected in the matter-of-fact style of the news stories. That particular selection of editorial and news scripts thus supported the critics of the editorials and confirmed the claims of the news department of success in holding off intrusions by the policy people.

Of the thirty editorials, fifteen were devoted to the Soviet Union or Soviet topics and another five to Soviet allies with mention of the USSR or the Soviet bloc. A further six dealt with Soviet allies without reference to their relations with Moscow. The four editorials that dealt with subjects other than the Soviet Union and the nations aligned with it included one about the Pulitzer prize going to a small Georgia newspaper, two about Libya, and one about China.

The choice of words in editorials describing Chinese and Soviet Communism show how important the state of U.S. relations seemed to be for the writers. An editorial on the president's trip to China said the United States would continue to deal with the issues that arise from the differences between the two countries. "One of those differences is the political and economic systems under which our peoples live. In all America's foreign relations, we have made no secret of our belief that everyone benefits from liberty, respect for human rights, and democratic self-government. But no nation knows better than ours that peoples of many different views can work together for the common good."

Two days later, the subject and the tone changed: "Human rights abuses are not a subject the Soviet Union wants its people to think too much about. Its elitist Party rule depends upon the suppression of free speech, free assembly, free press—indeed, free anything that promotes independence of mind and spirit. This is particularly true of the Baltic states of Latvia, Lithuania, and Estonia, where Soviet rule itself is based on a lie: the secret protocols attached to the von Ribbentrop–Molotov pact of 1939, in which the Soviet Union and Nazi Germany got together and agreed to halve Europe between them. But from the Soviets' point of view, suppression of human rights is not enough. To maintain its charade, the Kremlin also suppresses news of its repressive activities."

Other editorials on the Soviet Union seemed to make a special point of attacking its leader by name: "Judging from Soviet Party chief Konstantin Chernenko's recent speech on economic development, he's a man who doesn't want to be confused with the facts." "A lot of people just don't like rock music, and Soviet Party boss Konstantin Chernenko seems to be one of them."

There were some inconsistencies that regular listeners might have caught, including the glaring one in two editorials broadcast two weeks apart: "Today, Americans observe Law Day. It's an occasion for us to remember how essential law is to the preservation of our liberties. Observance of the law by citizens and officials, and impartial enforcement of law by government—these are foundations upon which a just society is founded." The editorial then went on to criticize the Soviet abuse of law. Two weeks earlier, the Voice had broadcast: "The United States has no intention of allowing Nicaragua, or any other Marxist state, to mask their aggressions behind false protestations of respect for the principles of rights and justice upon which the democratic world is based. That's why, last week, when it appeared that Nicaragua would try to put on a masquerade at the UN's World Court, we refused."

VOA news, by contrast, was straightforward and moderate in tone, even when covering Soviet events: "President Reagan says he is deeply concerned about Soviet dissident Andrei Sakharov and his wife, Yelena Bonner, both of whom are on hunger strikes in Gorky. He refused to be more specific at his news conference, saying anything he might say could harm her chances of getting permission to leave the Soviet Union for medical treatment."

It also routinely carried items that the administration might prefer not to have broadcast, including one about a congressional subcommittee finding that William Casey, director of the Central Intelligence Agency, had received campaign documents from the Carter administration while managing the Reagan campaign. (Voice editors did manage to put that item fourteenth on one newscast examined, behind such news as the visit to Moscow of Kim Il Sung, the North Korean leader, and the funeral of the queen of Thailand.) But the main point is that a story most people would consider unfavorable to the Reagan administration was broadcast in the same detail NBC or CBS would carry, as part of a proud record of VOA objectivity that was bent a bit on Vietnam but managed Watergate with hardly a slip.

Such objectivity is attacked by many émigrés, who say that by broadcasting news about shortcomings in the United States, the VOA wastes their tax dollars, since it is only doing the work of Radio Moscow. Others don't like the Voice's American emphasis. Telling and retelling the story of American living standards and political freedom has diminishing returns with Soviet listeners, in this view. The news department's even-handed reporting of the Soviet Union, other critics among the émigrés say, does not take into consideration the special nature of the Soviet regime, which does not deserve to be treated like Sweden or Brazil. The station must become more aggressive, this line goes, because that is the language the Soviet leaders understand.

Is it the only language they understand? veteran broadcasters at the VOA ask. These officials, who asked not to be identified, put these further questions to their critics: Are we to be an anti-Soviet station, or are we employed to use our talent and technology to tell the world about the American experience, flaws and all? Are we to make our impact on the Soviet people and their regime by becoming more like that regime in censoring and slanting our broadcasts? As to telling and retelling the story of America, that can be more powerful than a stack of editorials, in the view of one Voice official: "Of course some émigrés want us to broadcast to the Soviet workers to throw off their chains. We are caught between such wishes and static from the Democrats about presenting Reaganism as Americanism. If we tell the American story properly, that should satisfy both. Broadcasting a story about a strike at General Motors—the stronghold of capitalism—that's talking about America, but what an impression it makes on a listener in the Soviet Union."

The controversy over the role of the VOA seems mild compared to the problems of Radio Liberty. Whether conservative or liberal is in charge, there is no question of the Voice of America's commitment to democracy. But there have been instances of Radio Liberty broadcasts that were "anti-democratic, anti-Western and lending encouragement to xenophobic and aggressive attitudes which exist in the Soviet population," in the words of a staff report to the Board for International Broadcasting. According to William Korey, director of international policy research for B'nai B'rith International, another RL broadcast in the Ukrainian-language service contained anti-Semitic views. A Senate Foreign Relations Committee staff member reported that RL had hired or given additional freelance work to six reputed former members of the NTS, an émigré organization with anti-democratic tendencies and past anti-Semitic associations.

No one in any position of authority at Radio Liberty condones such broadcasts. But there are many who defend the methods of operation that permitted individual émigré broadcasters to produce such examples. One imagines former Soviet citizens to be anti-Communist, but why should they oppose the West and its democratic institutions? The opposite of Communism is not necessarily a system with a Congress, a president, and a Supreme Court. The Soviet regime and many of the men and women it forced into exile are in agreement in rejecting Western values. When the latter talk of overthrowing the former, they do not want a return to the brief period of Russian democracy, but to an older historical model of authoritarian rule, stressing Christian values and having little place for other beliefs.

The broadcast cited by Korey was of the memoirs of a Ukrainian official opposed to the Bolsheviks in the 1919–1920 civil war. The pogroms that took place then resulted from the "radicalism and fanaticism of the Jewish youth" supporting the Bolsheviks, it said. "The aggressiveness of volunteer Jewish detachments" made it "difficult to restrain the indignation of the Cossacks," some of whom "saw in every Jew [their] enemy." As Korey noted in the *Christian Science Monitor*, this blaming the victim has long been a staple of the anti-Semitic propaganda work of the Soviet regimes. Inside and outside Radio Liberty, the broadcast had a devastating effect, exacerbating the differences between the Russian nationalists and the liberal, mostly younger and Jewish faction. Jewish émigrés at the station were outraged. To them, the broadcast was the culmination of all the negative trends they had been opposing.

Examples were cited in reports on RL's broadcasting compiled in 1981 and 1983. In the first, James Critchlow, a veteran former RL staff member, monitored Russian broadcasts for a week in his capacity as planning and research officer for the Board for International Broadcasting. One, he found, advanced the authoritarian views of the nineteenth-century public figure Boris Chicherin. The broadcast said: "The abstract political principle of democracy . . . leads to domination of the majority by the minority. Chicherin believed this to be the fatal flaw of democracy and the root of all its evils." A broadcast on a nineteenth-century anti-czarist officer group, the Decembrists, maintained that what was "ominous in the Decembrist movement was the democratic and socialist tendency." A current affairs broadcast depicted "contemporary Western society [as] impotent to put an end to the terror [in] Italy and Germany."

The 1983 study compiled by Geryld Christianson, staff member of the Senate Committee on Foreign Relations, cited a Radio Liberty broadcast of a Solzhenitsyn speech accusing the United States of insisting that Taiwan institute "democracy bordering on chaos, on state treason, on the right to freely destroy one's country, the way Western countries allow it at home."

RL had originally scheduled a panel to discuss the Solzhenitsyn speech, but George Bailey, the American journalist and writer who became director of the station after the Reagan administration took office, ordered that part of the broadcast canceled, because he said its quality was not up to RL standards. He insisted to Christianson that the Solzhenitsyn speech was too important to be ignored by the station, but conceded that if he had to do it over again, he would not broadcast such a program without the balance of a commentary.

These disputes about the kinds of programs the United States ought to be broadcasting to the Soviet Union go back centuries in Russian history, to differences between the Westernizers and the Slavophiles. As the two forces emerged in mid-nineteenth-century Russia, some of the Slavophiles were preaching the superiority of traditional Russian civilization, supporting autocracy and opposing political participation, although others did back the idea of the *Zemsky Sobor*, an ancient popular assembly, and wanted to free the serfs and abolish censorship. The Westernizers thought that technology and democratic institutions were the path out of Russia's backwardness.

Contemporary spiritual descendants of the more reactionary Slavophiles have the advantage of being able to point to the mess the West has made of its societies, despite or perhaps because of technology and democracy. The Soviet Union, they say, is fortunate because the Communists have kept it backward. Now it can build its own institutions, different from those introduced by Lenin, but also from those of Jefferson.

These opinions are widely shared among exiles, with Solzhenitsyn and the writer Vladimir Maksimov the most prominent spokesmen, and also by a widening circle of thinkers and ordinary people in the Soviet Union, including many in the Party.

"Public opinion in the Soviet Union is heading in some strange directions, neither Western nor Communist," an editor prominent in New York émigré circles said. "We see a nationalism, perhaps encouraged by the regime, which doesn't know how to deal with it, and is putting out large, expensive printings of some nationalist books that Solzhenitsyn and Maksimov would approve of.

"They're turning back to an idea that has prevailed in Russia for centuries: it may not be good, but it's ours. It's linked to the remains of the Orthodox church. A quarter of the babies born in Moscow are baptized—and by couples who don't know anything about Jesus Christ or the scriptures, but do know, from their new access to information, that the Communist Party lies, and that their lives are not going to get better. They've given up the faith of the return of 'true Leninism' that was believed in until about twenty years ago. They've given up on attaining Western living standards, as Khrushchev promised. They think that something else, neither Communist nor Western, and not necessarily modern, lies before Russia. I wouldn't want to live in such a Russia, and I don't think the United States would be any better off at all with such a Russia."

But the United States is spending close to one hundred million dollars a year on a broadcast operation that not only airs the views of the anti-Western movement but quotes some of the least attractive representatives Russian nationalism has produced. Konstantin Pobedonostsev, the reactionary, anti-Semitic adviser to Czar Alexander III, is described in one broadcast as "a great conservative ideologist." The civil war general Wrangel, who once had 270 Red Army officers summarily shot, is chided for his excesses but praised for fighting to "defend the last clump of Russian land where justice and truth exist." The World War II general A. A. Vlasov, who collaborated with the Nazis and organized an army against the Soviet forces, is given a favorable image on RL broadcasts, Christianson says.

Radio Liberty's regulations would seem to rule out such broadcasts. RL is "committed to the principles of democracy." It is to "espouse no single specific political, economic, or religious creed," and it is told that "historical events should be approached in a critical as well as a tolerant spirit, avoiding chauvinistic or sectarian bias." Congress has decreed that RL operate "in a manner not inconsistent with the broad foreign policy objectives of the United States." It is not to permit its programs "to become the vehicles for any single point of view."

How is it possible for the broadcasts cited to have been made? A failure of management, in the assessment of a broadcast executive no longer connected with RL. George Bailey had some credentials as a journalist, but no experience as a manager. Moreover, he had been closely associated with the Russian nationalist writer Maksimov. Maksimov, who had been active in Soviet dissident circles, was forced into exile and settled in Paris. There he became editor of *Kontinent*, the émigré journal published with the financial help of Axel Springer Verlag, a West German publishing concern whose anti-communism is symbolized by the placement of its skyscraper headquarters along the Berlin wall. Bailey, who had been employed by Springer for twenty years, became the Springer representative on the editorial board of *Kontinent*.

There was widespread concern among the moderate faction at RL that Bailey's appointment would increase the influence of authoritarian and nationalist elements and decrease theirs. A June 1983 broadcast presenting Maksimov's views seemed to confirm these fears. As Christianson describes the broadcast, "the transcript of this program revealed that the form of government advocated by Maksimov had no room for Western-style elections. . . . Maksimov's blueprint appeared to be an iteration, conscious or not, of the program of the émigré National Labor Union–Solidarists party (NTS), an organization described in a 1955 Rand Corporation study as having 'totalitarian and anti-democratic tendencies.' Maksimov has had his differences with the NTS, even when collaborating with its members. It is entirely possible, however, that he has been influenced, perhaps unwittingly, by the NTS program. . . . Many of his own views are convergent with those of the NTS."

Bailey described the broadcast to Christianson as one advocating a kind of Swiss cantonal government and said no listener could have concluded that the program was critical of democracy. Earlier, when asked by the authors of an article on RL that appeared in *The Washington Post* about his connections to Maksimov, he had acknowledged his friendship and former business association but denied that Maksimov would have any influence on RL policies. Yet, as Christianson reported to the Senate Foreign Relations Committee, "I was told by one RL staffer that Mr. Bailey has placed on the staff of the Russian service four members of Maksimov's *Kontinent* magazine staff, added a freelancer from *Kontinent*, and given another *Kontinent* staff member additional freelance assignments. All were either members of the NTS or had close contacts with it. They were required to resign as NTS members as a condition of employment, since RL's guidelines forbid institutional relationships with any political parties or exile organizations. Whether their change of employment has changed their views seems questionable."

At the heart of the matter, according to a broadcast executive familiar with the dispute, is Bailey's belief that the layers of American administrative control that used to be imposed on the émigré broadcasting was demoralizing to the émigrés. They considered it a form of censorship not unlike the kind they had fled, and as long as it existed, there was a damper on their initiative and creativity. They accused the Americans who were fluent in Russian of not knowing enough about Soviet society, and the others of not knowing enough Russian to be effective. The result was a kind of internal competition, with the Americans looking over the shoulders of the émigrés, and the émigrés doing less than their best because of their resentment. There would be coups and countercoups; bright new staff members with lots of ideas would find themselves shunted into insignificant work. Radio Liberty had an underground telegraph worthy of any in the Soviet Union to report all this. Visitors would be greeted with the latest factional lineups.

Bailey restored the morale of at least one faction, the nationalists, but in giving them a freer hand he surrendered much of the control, in the view of this official. Christianson's report draws the same conclusion: "A new climate of deregulation has permeated the radios, either with the encouragement or the acquiesence of the Board for International Broadcasting members. The prevailing management attitude appears to be that if programmers are subject to fewer restraints and second-guessing on what they produce, they will be more creative, and that would outweigh the potential negative impact on the radios' credibility."

Critchlow of the BIB, who recommended in 1981 that every Russian broadcast be reviewed and approved in writing by a member of the "American management team" in *advance* of broadcast, said three years later that not only had this recommendation been ignored, but also that broadcast review had been so weakened as to be almost meaningless.

Controls seem to pose no such problem for Radio Liberty's Western competitors on the shortwave frequencies to the Soviet Union. VOA editors say that it has always been taken for granted that its Russian service and broadcasts in other Soviet languages are under American supervision. The Voice has managed to keep itself free from most exile disputes in this way (although not from those between Congress and the White House) and finds that morale hasn't suffered. The difference, according to those familiar with both stations, is that the Russian and other Soviet language broadcasts are the raison d'être of RL, while the services to the Soviet Union are only a part—important, but not the whole operation—of VOA's activities. Control at the Voice is not as strict as that advocated for RL; more emphasis is put on selecting the right people and making sure that the chain of command permits no slips. The Voice has found it possible to hire Americans who speak Russian and the other Soviet languages not only as supervisors but as lower-level management and even announcers. "We're the American radio," a VOA manager said. "They think they're the Russian radio. That's the difference." "We can't expect our higher-level people to read every word that's broadcast," another staff member said. "By that time, anyway, the damage has been done. What we can do is to make sure that exile politics plays no role—that this is an American operation."

The British Broadcasting Corporation's Russian service uses the same standards. Britons are in charge of the service at the top and secondary levels; the BBC prides itself on tight controls over what is broadcast. Britons make the policy and write the scripts. Native Russian speakers translate them and broadcast them. They are told when they are first hired that they are not working for an anti-Soviet station but for an independent, government-chartered British one. The exiles soon learn not to embellish their broadcasts with anti-Soviet ad libs, thanks to an effective system of monitoring and control.

One point frequently made to Soviet émigrés in Britain and their allies in Parliament is that the BBC's news coverage and commentary reflect the world, not just one part of it. For this reason, the BBC refused to broadcast reviews or excerpts of dissident literature in its Russian service unless the books had been translated and had made a mark in the world at large, not only the émigré community.

The BBC's even-handedness is anathema to some of the émigrés, including Solzhenitsyn, who decided to try to do something about it in a 1975 visit to the BBC External Services headquarters in London. It was an event that is still talked about in the BBC. Solzhenitsyn had been invited to make a broadcast. But he also requested a meeting with BBC management to see if he could put the Russian service on the right track. Speaking for an hour and a half from meticulously prepared notes, he attacked BBC policy and practices on a wide range of issues. The common theme was that the rulers of the Soviet Union were usurpers who had to be attacked. Until BBC programmers understood this, they would not be effective in reaching Soviet audiences.

As Solzhenitsyn spoke, the BBC executives present marveled at his eloquence and magnificent presence, but found it possible to accept only one of his recommendations. He had described the plight of religious believers in the Soviet Union in dramatic terms, telling how they were sometimes unable to find a place of worship within a hundred miles because of the regime's attacks on the church. Foreign broadcasts of religious services and commentary made a difference, he said, and ought to be stepped up. The BBC agreed.

An interesting sidelight of the visit was that Solzhenitsyn refused to meet with Anatoly Goldberg, the Russian-born commentator whose popularity in the Soviet Union was based in large part on his tolerance and his knowledgeable but restrained commentaries on the foibles of the Soviet system.

A month after the meeting, Solzhenitsyn wrote the head of external broadcasting to demand to know the reason his other recommendations hadn't been carried out. As one of those present at the meeting said, for the BBC to have acceded would have meant substituting a single point of view for the BBC mission of trying to present a fair and objective picture of world events.

Those at the BBC and VOA concede that their roles in the international broadcasting spectrum are different from Radio Liberty's. Even though RL's statement of mission says it is neither American radio nor exile radio, but international radio, its job is really perceived by all concerned as a surrogate for the censored and controlled Soviet media. This may rule out some of the broader perspectives of the BBC and VOA. But there is no reason that such a role cannot be compatible with some system of control over what the émigrés are broadcasting in the name of the American people.

Radio Liberty may be criticized in Washington and Paris, but it can point to one enthusiastic endorsement of its effectiveness— from the Soviet Union. Since the day RL first went on the air, its broadcasts have been subjected to continuous and thorough Soviet jamming. When Khrushchev and Brezhnev suspended jamming of other Western stations, Radio Liberty was always the exception.

This is because RL has taken on the task of informing people in the Soviet Union about the news that affects their lives, whether about the local economy or their government's actions abroad. It broadcasts twenty-four hours a day to the Soviet Union in Russian and a total of forty-three hours daily in fourteen of the other languages spoken in the USSR. Much of the programming is repeated because of the jamming; RL listeners often get (and need) six chances to hear the same program. The Voice of America, which also repeats its programs, broadcasts twenty-four hours a day in English and Russian. In addition to its round-the-clock English broadcasts, the BBC has five hours of Russian-language broadcasting every day. West Germany's Deutsche Welle broadcasts three hours daily in Russian. In addition, Soviet citizens listen regularly to the Voice of Israel, the Vatican Radio, and Radio Sweden; some have plotted out complex schedules of waveband switching, and get all of these stations on a single evening, plus Radio Peking.

One longtime Soviet listener considers the Voice of America and the BBC more like news agencies or headline services. They carry Soviet news only when it is of world importance. Radio Liberty, on the other hand, looks at the world from a Soviet citizen's viewpoint. It is a role the Soviet domestic media have forfeited, RL programmers say. By focusing on the Soviet Union, their radio can provide listeners not only uncensored news, but the cultural, political, and historical information the Soviet government blanks out. A large proportion of RL's one thousand non-technical personnel are former Soviet citizens who understand this culture and history; many are prominent writers, historians, and journalists.

Or renegades, as Soviet officials in charge of countering Radio Liberty and the other Western stations call them. The Soviet Union is believed to have three thousand jamming transmitters and as many as fifteen thousand technicians working on the task of silencing or distorting the voices from the West.

Jamming is outlawed by international conventions, and the Soviet Union never admits it is using it, although anyone turning on a radio inside or near Soviet borders could hardly miss the evidence. On the other hand, Soviet officials say every nation has the right to protect its citizens against hostile propaganda, particularly since they give foreign broadcasts all or part of the blame in the authoritative accounts of the three uprisings in Eastern Europe that required the intervention of Soviet troops. The workers' protests in East Berlin in 1953, in this view, were solely the result of propaganda and secret instructions broadcast by the West. The Hungarian uprising of 1956 had some local support, officials concede, but would not have been possible without the guidance and organization of Radio Free Europe's broadcasts. In 1968, the Czech and Slovak liberals were similarly blamed for anti-Sovietism and "creeping counter-revolution," but Soviet officials maintain that their weaknesses were exploited by the radio saboteurs who wanted to cause conflict between Moscow and Prague and to export counter-revolution from West to East.

There have been intermittent periods totaling about thirteen years when the Russian language broadcasts of the Voice of America and BBC could be heard without interference in the Soviet Union. Jamming of the Voice was stopped when Khrushchev toured the United States in 1959 and again in the years of détente in the early 1970s. An event like an invasion or the crisis in Poland brings it back. American broadcasters say the Soviet government spends more each year on jamming than the U.S. government does for all the operation of the Voice and Radio Liberty. Listeners in the Soviet Union are more concerned with how to defeat the jamming.

Many Soviet listeners understand the technology of jamming and know how to take advantage of its limitations. Jamming is accomplished by broadcasting electronically generated noise, white sound, tapes of other broadcasts, or multiple echoes of incoming transmissions. Ground-wave transmitters are used in cities and other concentrations of population. They can blanket an area effectively, but their range is limited to about twenty miles. Sky-wave jammers bounce signals off the ionosphere hundreds or thousands of miles from the area to be jammed. These distorting signals override the broadcasts beamed to those areas.

Listeners cope with the ground-wave jammers simply by leaving the area of their coverage. Going to the beach, or out in a boat, or to a country house has a value beyond recreation in the Soviet Union. One consideration in a decision to save up money for a dacha is the advantage of weekends on which it is possible to catch up on the uncensored news of the world. With smaller and better transistor radios, a house isn't necessary; a picnic in the woods will do. The friends of an intellectual who lives in a town outside Leningrad (and outside the ground-wave jamming radius) know that they shouldn't call him between four and six P.M., because that's when he listens to the BBC.

Sky-wave jammers also have their gaps. There are changes in the ionosphere when the sun has set in the East but is still shining in the West. This means that the incoming broadcasts can be shielded from some of the jamming by what Western broadcasters call "twilight immunity." Their broadcast schedules take advantage of this effect, as do the listening schedules of knowledgeable Soviet citizens.

Despite the practice of listening to foreign broadcasts openly in places like the Baltic beaches, the Western stations can sometimes cause trouble for Soviet citizens who aren't cautious enough. It is not against the law to tune in to a foreign station, but it is illegal to spread propaganda hostile to the Soviet state. Ivanov is thus permitted to spend as many hours as he wants listening to and absorbing what the authorities call the psychological warfare of the West against the progressive forces of the East. The minute he starts to talk about it with Petrova, he may be in trouble. The authorities usually react in more subtle ways than outright legal action. Files are compiled on those known to be regular short-wave listeners, either on the basis of eavesdropping neighbors' reports or on conversations about the broadcasts. This information is normally paid little attention. But if it is combined with other circumstances, such as suspicion of passing along samizdat material, it can be held against the suspect.

How many listen? Accurate figures are hard to come by, since the BBC or Voice of Israel cannot conduct listenership surveys in the Soviet Union, and letters from Soviet listeners addressed to foreign stations sometimes get diverted. Radio Liberty's surveys show almost seven million daily listeners in the Soviet Union, despite jamming so intense that one listener said he had to sit through four or five consecutive newscasts to be able to make sense out of a single item. The BBC estimates its regular listeners at five percent of the adult population. Some survey research is possible in the West, and these figures are based on that work. Specialists question Soviet travelers and émigrés and compare notes with Western diplomats who move in official Soviet circles. Their conclusions are that about a third of the Soviet population listens to foreign broadcasts on a fairly regular basis. Among those whose views were sought for this book, all reported at least occasional listening, and most had listened frequently or regularly. The Voice of America and the BBC competed for top spot in their preferences, with Deutsche Welle close behind, and Radio Liberty cited much less often because of the jamming.

The engineers and communications specialists in the West who are working on technological methods of combating jamming concede that they may be like the generals whose plans are based on how they fought the last war. The dramatic growth of other kinds of information reaching Soviet men and women in the next decade may make jamming as relevant as the Maginot Line.

· 7 ·

The Borscht Pot Antenna

When Andrei Sakharov boldly wrote an appeal on a blackboard during an international genetics symposium in Moscow to protest the imprisonment of Zhores Medvedev, the dissident scientist, in a psychiatric hospital, he was able to reach only those in the hall with his words: "Academician A. D. Sakharov is in the auditorium collecting signatures for a protest against the committal of Zhores Medvedev to a mental hospital," and to collect only a few signatures. The signatures and Sakharov's other activities did help in securing Medvedev's eventual release. But what if Sakharov had been able to enter his appeal into a computer terminal connected with hundreds of universities and scientific institutes across the nation, in a network like those routinely used by U.S. scientists, and within seconds have it on screens and being printed out, giving other scientists the opportunity to respond immediately on the same network, in a kind of electronic petition?

Computers linked in networks are among the many technological developments already in place in the West that will change the way the Soviet state functions when they are finally accepted by a reluctant Party. Their application in science and the military is already well along, but very little has been done to use computers to modernize the management of the huge state economy. When this does happen, and the new technology moves outside the laboratories and institutes, access will be multiplied many times. This will have profound effects on the way information is exchanged, not only for the needs of the state, but in the interests of the next generation of Sakharovs opposing the state's right to decide what can be written and spoken.

A future Sakharov would have many ways of reaching a wide audience with his or her human rights appeals. They could be relayed on a videotelephone system like the one now being developed in Great Britain. They could be televised into Soviet homes from satellites, either from a video Voice of America or by the overspill of a signal footprint from a satellite broadcasting to Western Europe or Japan. They could be picked up by home hobby shop equipment, perhaps with a dish antenna made from borscht pots or other metal scrap, and taped for use on home videocassette players. They might be passed along by the wireless telephones being developed by Soviet engineers, which would mean less danger of tapping.

But not only the dissidents will be affected by the technological changes that will take place in the Soviet Union. Everyone will have a better chance at being better informed, and as a result the regime may decide that its media will have to be a little bit more straightforward and complete. The underground information networks described in this book will change in two ways: their capacity will increase, but, in the long run, there may be slightly less need for them if the official information systems become somewhat more honest.

Many of the products of Western technological research are unsuited for Soviet society the way it is now constituted and is likely to be for some time. A third of the population of the United States owns personal computers or has plans to buy them. "But ordinary Soviet men and women don't need PCs as Americans do," an émigré who specializes in high technology said. "There's not much demand yet. What could a Soviet do with a PC? Figure his income tax? Balance her checkbook? Keep track of his stock prices? They don't have any of that." For this reason, the commercial American computer networks, which permit subscribers to shop and bank at home, would have limited use.

Scientific and academic networks are another matter. The United States has many such networks, including CSNET, which connects institutions doing computer research, COGNET, for those engaged in research in cognitive science, and BITNET, an organization of twenty-one universities from California to New York. BITNET members can send each other electronic mail from home, office, or laboratory terminals. The information exchanged ranges from little personal notes left on distant screens to entire research proposals, computer programs, and manuscripts. BITNET has an electronic bulletin board, BITSERVE, which stores announcements of conferences, requests for information, and a directory of experts willing to be contacted at their terminals.

The applications for a BITNET in a country as vast as the Soviet Union are easy to see. But the regime can see the disadvantages, too, and as a result progress in computer networking has been very slow and hedged with many restrictions. "The existence of a network of word processors, personal computers and electronic mail would pose a near-impossible challenge for the police and their political control," Marshall Goldman, the Harvard specialist on the Soviet economy, has written. "If even now copying machines are viewed as a threat to the political security of the country, word processors and interactive computers, with their potential for underground communications, would be even more of a problem."

Loren Graham, whose specialty at the Massachusetts Institute of Technology is Soviet science and technology, says the Soviet regime is meeting this challenge by insisting that all computers be housed in institutions, not home offices. If decentralization were permitted, he wrote, no printers would be provided for the home computers; disks would have to be taken to the office to be printed. Another method would be to connect all the outlying microcomputers to the central office, which would record all the material they produced. Unplugging the home computer from this monitoring would put it out of action.

"All this suggests that the Soviets will have unusual difficulties adjusting to the computer revolution," Graham has written. "Complete computer systems and access to international telecommunications networks will not be placed in the hands of individual citizens. The Soviet Union will not be able to keep up with the pace of development of computers and the widening of information access in the West. The civilian computer technology that is now penetrating to the lowest level of society—the individual—

will give a real advantage to societies which do not try to control information."

Besides losing the benefits of mass production economies in producing small computers, the Soviet Union will also "pay a stiff price by severely limiting the rapidity of growth of the computer culture, by hampering the spread of computer literacy among their young people," Graham maintains. "Furthermore, the Soviet authorities can never be sure that some smart kid will not defeat their controls and break out of the central computer surveying his activities. If he succeeds, by definition he does not leave traces."

Western computer specialists have lots of suggestions for their Soviet colleagues planning ways to beat the system. If printers are banned, a computer tinkerer would not have much trouble rigging an electric typewriter to his or her terminal as a slow-speed alternative. On Taiwan, where an advancing computer society coexists uneasily with an authoritarian government, monitors come around at the end of each working day to check what has been produced on institutional computers. But researchers dealing with sensitive issues have plenty of time before that to print out anything controversial and erase it from their machines.

Another blueprint for the future expansion of the individual's communication possibilities in the Soviet Union can be seen in the cable systems being installed or planned in the West. European models go considerably beyond the American use of cable, which is mostly a means of getting better or different television pictures. Europe has long had videotext services, but such an innovation in the Soviet Union would be easy to censor and control. Not so the person-to-person information systems being built into the next generation of European cable. West Germany's $125 million Bigfon system will use fiber-optic lines to link six cities. Home viewers will receive not only television but facsimile transmissions on their screens. The same lines will carry videotelephone images; West Germans will be able to make picture phone calls for four to five times the price of an ordinary call.

In Great Britain, the government's master plan for wiring the nation is based on the position that cable must provide many more services than it does in the United States. Kenneth Baker, the minister for information technology, wants a system that can, among other functions, relay the text of a printed page from any five thousand subscribers to any other five thousand subscribers of the service in three seconds.

If such a system ever reaches the Soviet Union, the regime would have to add five thousand censors to its calculations. Its policy to date has been simply to turn its back on such advances, considering the risks not worth the advantages. But the policy has diminishing returns, in the view of Graham of MIT: "Whether the Soviets can maintain their international status atop an already backward economy that falls increasingly behind a computer-dominated world must be a profoundly troubling question for the rulers in Moscow."

BITNET has plans to make use of IBM's international network, VNET, to expand its information exchanges to other countries. The benefits to the Soviet Union of such a link-up would be enormous. Its specialists could tap the experience of the computer science departments of MIT, Columbia, Stanford, and Harvard, as well as other departments and IBM's research center. A Soviet BITNET might also have unintended effects, says Vice Chancellor Ira Fuchs of the City University of New York, a BITNET founder: "Something interesting happens sociologically when communication becomes easier and freer. IBM found it out with its internal system. VNET became gripenet."

It is easy to understand the impact of television broadcast accessibility to Soviet viewers if one compares what Soviet and Western stations are offering on an average evening. The best place to watch is in Estonia's lovely capital, Tallinn, where the signal from Finland's two channels comes across the Baltic into Soviet homes. Reception is not perfect, but it is clear enough. The difference in content makes the occasional fuzziness and audio noise seem unimportant. The evening begins on the Soviet programs with a rerun of a youth-oriented film, followed by more youth and children's programming, including a film about Baltic beaches. "Actual Camera," a local features program, is followed by the national news, "*Vremya*." A film about World War II ends the evening. Tallinn has four channels, one in the Estonian language and three in Russian. On the evening chosen, the other channels are carrying hockey, a health program, basketball championships, "Uneasy Heart," a youth-oriented musical, "Good Night for the Little Ones," an installment of the serial film "Courage," weightlifting, the Moiseyev dance troupe, and a "Telespectacular" of Soviet variety acts.

A click of the channel selector on sets that have undergone a simple modification brings in Finland—or rather, the world. Old movies from the United States, British music hall shows, German cabaret, Swedish nature programs fill Helsinki's evenings. One typical schedule began with a six P.M. serial about the adventures of an American Indian tribe. Rock music from Sweden followed, and then a British mystery. There was Finnish news and weather, followed by a Doris Day film from the 1950s. On the second channel, "Top Hits from Eurovision," the Western European TV network, was followed by a concert and profile of Boris Vian, a French protest singer.

An Estonian professor who says he prefers to watch the local channels considers Finnish television a direct line to the United States and all of its bad influence. Without too much discretion, he says, the Finnish television producers warehouse American sitcoms and films and pass over some of the best Western Europe has to offer (a check of programs for a month did not confirm this second point; Helsinki viewers were getting some very worthwhile offerings from Britain and the Continent). In any case, in the professor's view, access to broadcasts from the West results in a very low standard of programming. Mature Soviet citizens can deal with it, but the youth cannot, which is one reason Estonia's official channels run so much programming for youth.

But a former correspondent for the Finnish television news department said Estonian viewers, although they may enjoy the Western comedies, pay particular attention to the news and public affairs programs. When the correspondent visited Estonia as a tourist, he was surprised to find himself being treated like a movie star. People would come up to him in the street and tell him how much they enjoyed his reporting from Western capitals.

An Estonian student said he watched the first political debate in his life on Finnish television. President Carter was facing

Ronald Reagan, and the American television producers were showing both at once on a split screen. The Estonians could understand the Finnish subtitles, since that language is close to theirs, and some of the English Carter and Reagan were speaking. The student said it was a landmark in his life. Here was open competition for public office, something unheard of in his little nation for half a century. As an extra dividend, there was the technological achievement of the split screen.

The professor who doesn't like the Western programming (although he watches it regularly enough to be a very well-informed critic) conceded that its popularity has increased enrollment in Finnish language classes at Estonian universities. The students who sign up say they want to be more aware of the common Uralic roots of Finnish and Estonian. But they really want to be able to catch nuances in the broadcasts, he says.

But now technology has opened the way for all of the Soviet Union to be able to see the programs that were once confined to the small zones of reception along the borders. Tallinn, already a center for dissidents opposed to the Russification of Estonia and its population of 1.3 million, has become the unofficial video recording headquarters of the USSR. The best of Finnish (which can also mean American, British, Italian, German, or Brazilian) television is recorded in apartments where reception is the best. Sometimes Russian language voice-overs are added. The cassettes are distributed to Moscow, Leningrad, and other cities with no fear of border controls for those who carry them on Aeroflot planes from Tallinn; Estonia, willingly or not, is part of the Soviet Union.

The video-taping operation doesn't work as well in other areas of the Soviet Union able to pick up foreign television. Latvia and Lithuania can get strong Swedish signals across the Baltic, but not in a language readily understood. Viewers in the Ukraine and Byelorussia can watch Polish television. For a time, during the Solidarity period, that was particularly rewarding, but now the broadcasts differ little from the Soviet ones. To the south, citizens of the Moldavian SSR can watch and understand Romanian television, since their territory was once a part of Romania and they speak the same Romance language. That was once another window to the West in the days when Romanian president Nicolae

Ceaușescu appeared on the "Today" show and Western programs appeared on Romanian television. Ideological crackdowns have since limited the Romanian programmers' freedom.

Whatever the language difficulties, when a major news event takes place, the pictures often tell the story. The release of the dissident Bukovsky in 1976 is a good example. After thirteen years in labor camps and psychiatric hospitals, he was freed in exchange for the Chilean Communist leader Luis Corvalan, who had been imprisoned after the coup that deposed Salvador Allende. The Soviet government considered the exchange none of the business of its readers and viewers. To make it public would have acknowledged the existence of political prisoners in the Soviet Union as well as Chile. No word appeared in the Soviet press; there were even denials that such a deal could even be contemplated. But Finnish television broadcast footage of Bukovsky's arrival in the West as Corvalan reached Moscow. That video tape is a classic among dissidents.

Soviet citizens like such refreshing changes from the official news, but they are equally interested in relief from the tiresome diet of uplifting discussions, war movies, and what could be called peacetime war movies: the struggles to get the dam built, the land plowed, and the production quota met. There are struggles in James Bond films, *April in Paris*, and some of the other Western productions Finnish television shows, but it is also possible to watch them for half an hour or an entire evening without feeling preached to. For that reason, the videocassette black market has some surprising hits.

Video recorders cost as much as new cars in the Soviet Union, and are as much sought after as any shiny BMW in town. They are used for many purposes other than capturing news events like the Bukovsky release. For one thing, there is a language problem, and the Russian voice-overs on cassettes from Finnish TV are not widely available. "Most of us speak Beatles English but no more," a Moscow student admitted. Entertainment needs less knowledge of foreign languages than news and public affairs, and, in keeping with viewing patterns in countries where there is no need to worry about a policeman checking content, accounts for heavy VCR usage in the Soviet Union.

Having video tapes is not against the law, but their content may violate the laws against disseminating anti-Soviet propaganda. A political video tape could be expected to be dealt with far more severely than would a banned book. The new technology is much more effective as a propaganda tool. A dissident can lend a book to a friend, but can reach a whole roomful of friends at the same time with a cassette of a Western discussion of Sakharov's plight or Kremlin power struggles. The law makes no distinction between book and cassette, but dissidents believe that the prosecutors would.

Entertainment, with the possible exception of a political cabaret making fun of the Politburo, offers no such dangers. The three most popular categories of video in the underground viewing rooms are the Western films that don't get shown on Soviet television, pornography, and the innocuous entertainment programs Western European networks broadcast such as "Christmas in Bavaria" or the Swedish rock group Abba (once officially accepted in the Soviet Union but later banned after its participation in the United States Information Agency's "Let Poland be Poland" program).

The Soviet Union makes about 150 feature films a year and imports another 150. Only about fifteen of the imports are American and another fifteen or twenty British, French, West German, and Italian. The selection process is aimed at making sure that what gets into Soviet movie houses reflects unfavorably on Western society in some way. At the same time, the films must avoid scenes and ideas that would remind Soviet audiences of the inconsistencies in their regime's propaganda. This tends to restrict Soviet views of Western life. But the video recorder leaps the barrier, bringing into Soviet living rooms movies like *The Deer Hunter* and *Apocalypse Now*, to name two cited by dissidents as popular for showing both lots of action and some nuances about America at war.

The X-rated films from Scandinavia are recorded to avoid another barrier. The sexual revolution in the West, which created a large industry to produce pornography, passed the Soviet Union by, as have so many others.

"Christmas in Bavaria" requires more explanation. Snowflakes fall, the choir of an Alpine village church sings, pop stars in stylized mountain costumes join in. "It sounds corny, and it is," an émigré film critic said. "But it provides something that people really can't get from the official channels."

For that reason, and for the privilege of seeing Danish nudes and American tough guy movies without a moral, Soviet citizens pay as much as $250 a videocassette. The trade is brisk—how brisk, no one can measure. But it is clear that the tapes come from many sources in addition to the Finnish television transmissions that cross the Baltic. Finnish stations don't broadcast X-rated films; such videos have to be smuggled into the country. Many other kinds of tapes are brought from the United States and Western Europe, and not only by dissidents.

A certain discount jeans store a few blocks south of the United Nations on Manhattan's East Side has long been a favorite shopping place for Soviet diplomats and their families about to return home or go on leave. Now the electronics shops in the neighborhood and in midtown are getting business from the same clientele. They can buy the kind of video that will never be shown in the Soviet Union for twenty or thirty dollars, and a VCR for a tenth of the black market price in Moscow. Border controls do not constitute much of a problem for official travelers.

Why should the Soviet Union try to ban ordinary Western movies at all? *Dr. Zhivago* or pornography is one thing, but who cares whether simple entertainment programs from the West, or escapist adventure films, come into the country? There is no such thing as a neutral story, Soviet ideologists contend. Western filmmakers may pretend or even believe that they have no political message, but they are wrong, according to the Soviet critic Grigory Oganov: "When a nice-looking modern Cinderella with whom millions of young girls can easily identify themselves finds her capitalist wonderland prince; or when the cruel policeman of a TV serial is made into a public hero, when a wicked spy and killer is glorified as a rescuer of civilization, there is yet another juggling trick, where notions are manipulated like cards. That is how anti-Sovietism is being whipped up."

No figures are made public on the number of video recorders in Soviet homes. The black market price must be a limiting factor.

But as with every other technological development introduced from outside the country, the VCR count must be increasing rapidly. Americans bought six million of them in 1980 and ten million two years later. In televisions, radios, telephones, and audio tape recorders, Russian buying patterns have followed those of America.

The Soviet electronics industry began the manufacture of video tape recorders in the 1970s, but withdrew from the market in a few years because of complaints about the poor quality of its products. There was some suspicion that an official vision of technology out of control might also have played a role in the decision. But the audio tape recorder industry has flourished. Such recorders are far less complicated to manufacture, and although their role in the underground telegraph is no secret to the authorities, the impact of sound may be judged to be less than the combined sight and sound of video.

That was clearly not so on the summer day in 1980 when 15,000 Muscovites crowded the Taganka Square and the side streets around Yuri Lyubimov's avant-garde theater to pay tribute to its best-loved actor, Vladimir Vysotsky, who had died of a heart attack at the age of forty-two. Many in the crowd carried their tape recorders and played Vysotsky's hoarse-voiced ballads to each other as they wept for the man they loved as the authentic voice of the Soviet individual in an authoritarian system. Vysotsky wrote and sang about the ordinary situations and feelings of Soviet life. He treated factories as difficult and dismal places to work in, not as shrines to production. Unlike the official media, which all but ignores the existence of prisoners, criminal or political, he wrote about the labor camps and prisons. "What are you drinking out there?" one of his prisoners asks. "There's nothing but snow here, nothing to drink."

The regime first tried to ignore Vysotsky's ballads, but as the tapes made at concerts and café performances multiplied into the millions, it decided to issue some of the less controversial ones on the official Melodiya record label. They sold well, but the underground tapes also continued to flourish. A nationwide network for exchanging Vysotsky tapes sprang up. Some of his favorite ballads were re-recorded so often that the words became indistinct.

When Vysotsky died, the authorities tried the same tactics. There was no obituary notice in the national papers; the news was not carried on radio or television. This censorship was the rough equivalent of the United States' trying to hush up the death of John Lennon. Of course, it didn't work. Spreading the news of Vysotsky's death to the nation was the finest hour of the underground telegraph. It forced the regime to permit a public memorial service and viewing at the theater and to abandon its plans to have Vysotsky interred in another city, where there would have been no crowds and no displays of anti-regime emotion. And the crowded scene outside the Taganka was another triumph for the *magnitizdat* network of underground tapes. Weeping Vysotsky admirers were trading tapes as they waited at dawn for a chance to pass by his coffin.

Magnitizdat—a word combining the Russian for tape and publishing—was one of the reasons for a remarkable story of Soviet tape recorder production and sales. Fewer than half a million were produced in 1965, according to Soviet statistics,[11] but that figure had doubled by 1970 and doubled again in another five years. In the 1980s, the three-million mark was passed in annual production. No Soviet industry is going to mass produce equipment for dissidents. The tape recorder has a firm place in Soviet family life. It is used to record birthday and holiday greetings, to send oral letters (a simpler kind of electronic mail) to relatives in the military or at distant construction projects, to record the voices of children and favorite uncles at parties. Home studios record the efforts of youthful violinists as well as of rock groups and folk singers.

The tape recorders also work for the unofficial information system in two ways. They are the medium for storing and relaying the underground oral literature, the protest songs and poems of the successors to Vysotsky. They also capture and preserve some

11. First cited by Gene Sosin in Rudolph Tokes' *Dissent in the U.S.S.R.* (Charlotte: UMI Publications). Figures brought up to date by the author.

of the programs carried by the foreign broadcasts. Tape recorders go along on picnics, not only to play the songs that are never broadcast on Soviet stations, but to be coupled with shortwave radios. They record foreign broadcasts of news, commentary, and more forbidden music, with the signals clear because the picnic site is out of the reach of the city jammers. Both recorders and radios are commonplace at country dachas and vacation colonies. Even in the closely packed living space of union or enterprise vacation camps, the tape recorders can be used freely. There is no efficient way to check the content of the tapes brought along for the vacation or to tell whether new material is being added at night from the shortwave frequencies.

The audio tape libraries in Soviet homes are oriented toward music, some of the protest variety, but also some nice neutral selections to play when the radio is carrying nothing but production songs by trade union choruses. They also contain plain words: an underground ballad taped at a party, a poem taped from someone else's tape in a chain that could go back to a well-known dissident poet at home or in exile, and programs recorded from foreign broadcasts. The dissident author Georgi Vladimov says taped copies of President Reagan's statements on Soviet–American relations, broadcast by the Voice of America, circulate widely in the USSR. Radio Liberty broadcast *The Gulag Archipelago* in full—a feat that took seven hundred hours of air time. RL broadcasters are certain that it is all down on tape in many collections in the Soviet Union, and that these stacks of tapes serve as masters for anyone wishing to make a copy of an excerpt of the *Gulag* story, perhaps someone who had spent time in one of the camps Solzhenitsyn described or had relatives there.

It is possible to make good tapes from foreign shortwave broadcasts because of the great steps forward in radio technology of recent decades. At the same time, many more people are listening. The USSR had only 90 million radios in 1965, but by 1981 there were 168 million—more than one for every two people.

"The transistor revolution has been the most important development in mass communication in the past two decades," Douglas Muggeridge, managing director of the BBC's external broadcasting services, said.[12] "It has opened up new horizons for millions across the world. Less than thirty years ago, there were about 230 million radio sets in the world; today there are 1.5 billion.

"It was the development of the transistor which made light and portable radio sets a practical reality. Subsequent technological advances have made possible the production both of cheaper and more technically sensitive sets. The purchase of a radio is still a major undertaking for the less well-off in many parts of the world, but it is worth noting that the dramatic increase in set ownership over the past thirty years is even more marked in the developing world than in the developed. Nor should it be forgotten that group listening is common in many poorer areas."

Igor Reichlin listened to his first broadcasts on a heavy Telefunken radio his Soviet officer father had acquired in Germany after World War II. By the time he left the Soviet Union in 1981, exchanging the life of an Aeroflot employee and freelance writer for graduate study and a job with *The Wall Street Journal*, Soviet radios had contracted considerably in size and increased dramatically in number and power. Shortwave radios played a major role in this expansion because they provided the best means of communication for domestic stations across the Soviet land mass. Sixty million shortwave radios were in Soviet homes and work places in 1975, and production goals in the 1980s call for nearly doubling this number.

Reichlin says these sets are manufactured without the high frequency bands used by foreign broadcasters, but for a few rubles anyone can buy the necessary capacitor and transistors at an electronic hobby shop. Rewiring is not difficult; there is even space left for the modifications in the radio chassis. "One model of television set made in a factory in one of the Baltic republics can get Swedish and Finnish television without any modifications," he said. "As you can imagine, it's much in demand."

Soviet customers can pick up the kinds of large radio–tape recorders favored by Western youth if they want to pay the thou-

---

12. In a letter to the author.

sand-ruble (about $1,500 at official exchange rates) price at the state-run secondhand stores. At one such store in the Ukraine, clerks said the radios were brought in by Soviet sailors who had bought them in Japan and the West. The big instruments seem to be used more for home entertainment than listening to the West, but sometimes those two functions are the same.

Telephone technology in the Soviet Union lags behind that of the West, and politics keeps getting in the way of the engineers who are trying to catch up. There are 75 telephones for every 100 Americans (173 per 100 in Washington, telephone champion of the world). The Soviet figure is about 9 per 100. No one in the West is certain, because the Communication Ministry no longer reports figures for the annual survey compiled by AT&T, *The World's Telephones*. The number of telephones doubled between 1970 and 1979, and press reports have spoken of increasing production annually. There are 25 million calls made every day within Moscow, 1,264,000 domestic long-distance calls, and 2,280 foreign calls daily. The total of telephones in service is believed to be about 25 million. Soviet scientists have long made use of fiber-optic transmission and other new communications techniques, but mostly in the well-financed space program rather than on the ground. Touch-tone dial and electronic switching are also in the very early stages of development.

Nevertheless, the telephone network in the USSR has long since reached the point of size and complexity at which it is impossible to monitor the calls of individuals without making every other person a security agent. As the 1980 Moscow Olympics approached, dissidents and Western business people waited with equal anticipation for the introduction of directly dialed service abroad, which had been promised in time for the games. The dissidents saw the service as a speedy and more secure link in their loop of contacts with colleagues in foreign countries. The Westerners looked forward to an end to long waits to reach their home offices. Since the system helped speed foreign trade transactions and made the Soviet Union more competitive, the Westerners were certain that the regime would have to tolerate its abuse by the dissidents. As it turned out, they underestimated the ability of the Soviet regime to sacrifice reasonable, convenient practices when it considers its more important interests threatened.

Direct dialing lasted only two years. In the summer of 1982, Soviet operators began refusing to put through calls to foreign numbers that were not placed in the old-fashioned way. By that autumn, the direct dialing in the other direction, from the West and Japan, had been cut off. The number of international circuits was also reduced, from a high of twenty-seven for the United States in 1980 to nineteen in 1982. The Ministry of Communication said the service was interrupted because the equipment had to be overhauled. Very few people took this explanation seriously. It was clear to all involved—correspondents, business people, dissidents, and ordinary Soviet citizens with contacts abroad—that information control was the real purpose of the restrictions. The technology that enabled Pepsico in Purchase, New York, to dial its Moscow branch and talk about vodka-cola deals also enabled Ukrainian dissidents in Jersey City to dial their Kiev branch and discuss church closings and arrests. The trouble for the authorities was that the dissident affairs then became part of the information loop that disseminated the news to a broad audience in the USSR. Émigrés would provide Western wire services with the stories they had heard. The wire reports would reach the broadcast newsrooms of the Voice and BBC, and soon be on their way back to the Soviet Union.

Eliminating direct dialing didn't break the loop, but it did make it slower and more dangerous to use. The fiction of equipment malfunctions was exposed shortly after the ban went into effect, when Western businesses were permitted limited direct dialing from Moscow.

The effect of the ban on calls to and from the United States was immediately felt. As with the letter traffic, telephone calling had risen steadily in the 1970s, keeping pace with the increasing tide of emigration. About 39,000 calls were made in both directions in 1973. By 1978, the figure had reached 104,000, and three years later, in 1981, had more than doubled again to 243,000. The cutoff of direct dialing dropped it back to 204,000 in 1982.

It did not take long for Soviet foreign trade officials to get together with the security and telephone people to figure out a way to restore selective direct dialing. In the process, they settled a few political debts; the privilege was extended mainly to nationals of countries on good terms with Moscow. The offices of the Soviet foreign trade organizations and banks were the first to get outfitted with special automatic lines for international calls. Embassies came next, as Western business managers jockeyed for position on waiting lists. Then it was time for the rewards. West German business firms in Moscow were put at the top of the lists, presumably in recognition of the Bonn government's continued high level of trade with the Soviet Union and restraint in political discourse. The Americans, whose government was ranked low in both categories, continued to wait.

It is relatively easy to outmaneuver dissidents and slight political adversaries in an era of copper-wire telephone systems, but that era is swiftly coming to its end. Viktor Vasilyev, who heads the Moscow city telephone network, told a Soviet interviewer that in the next century, subscribers are likely to have tiny pocket-sized telephones they can take anywhere, without the need for wires. According to Gerard O'Neill, a Princeton physicist, Americans will not have to wait nearly that long for a satellite-linked transceiver, pocket-sized and powered by batteries, that can send messages anywhere in the continental United States in seconds. Arthur Clarke, who invented the communications satellite, is working on plans with UNESCO to help Third World nations leapfrog the copper-wire phase of telephone development. He foresees portable telephones so small they can be worn like wrist-watches, and powerful enough to reach a satellite 22,300 miles above the equator. If personal satellite communications is still very much in the planning stage, the use of optical fiber systems is here, permitting two thousand telephone calls to be carried simultaneously on two filaments of glass thinner than a human hair.

The Soviet press praises the work of the nation's scientists and engineers in fiber optics and satellite applications. But each step forward will have to be viewed with political as well as technical criteria. Will it be another way of breaking technological barriers to achieve better communication, or another danger to the state's information controls?

The attempt to maintain those controls is best illustrated by the effort put into one kind of technology, jamming, to defeat another kind, shortwave broadcasting. The methods and costs of jamming have already been detailed. The technologists in the West are working on ways to make radio more able to penetrate it, with some help from the diplomats.

For the first time, the International Telecommunications Union, the United Nations' broadcasting authority, has agreed to Western demands for regulations to permit broadcasters to get around jamming. The 1984 World Administrative Radio Conference listened to the thirty-five examples of worldwide jamming brought up by some of the 120 nations present and agreed that techniques such as switching frequencies and increasing transmitter power were justified in combating them. The ITU was instructed to help in the anti-jamming work. Switching frequencies and adding power makes the world's shortwave traffic even more heavy, but, as the West argued, so does jamming, which in addition is against the letter and spirit of several international agreements.

In the laboratories, work is in progress on jam-proof radio transmitters and other methods of overcoming the electronic interference. There has been talk among American and British broadcasters of restoring the old barrage system, in which Western stations synchronized their transmissions and frequencies and blanketed the airwaves so thoroughly that Soviet jammers could not drown them all out.

Another way of getting around jamming is simply by modernizing transmitting equipment. Voice of America officials said that when President Reagan came to their Washington studios to make a broadcast, he used the same equipment that President Eisenhower had used in the 1950s. Some of it required vacuum tubes rather than transistors. The tubes had to be sent to an old technician in Munich for replacement or repair. Reagan and the Voice joined in persuading Congress to appropriate more money to increase transmitter power. VOA officials say the increase cannot be canceled out by more Soviet jamming because even with the weak signals being broadcast for years, a great deal gets through. "They could build more big jammers," a VOA editor said. "But that is expensive, and would have to be paid for somewhere in their economy—twenty fewer cars coming off their assembly lines, perhaps."

Muggeridge says his service will continue to take jamming in stride: "I do not think the BBC should let the possibility of jamming by certain countries deter us from seeking to exploit the enormous possibilities that new technologies offer in the field of international broadcasting. We do not, after all, cease to broadcast in Russian or Polish because these happen, at the moment, to be jammed—indeed the fact that we do continue our broadcasts is not without significance."

The United States has perfected a satellite transmission system for FM radio signals that could reach every home in the Soviet Union with broadcasts as clear as those heard by American listeners to domestic FM stations. The FM or frequency modulation signal cannot normally travel very far, since it is limited to the area in the line of sight of its transmitter. There would be no line-of-sight obstacles between the satellite and the radio receivers on the ground in the USSR. Technicians say there is a choice between a stationary satellite at the 22,300-mile height or of a satellite a few hundred miles up that would sweep across the Soviet land mass every twenty minutes.

Such a signal would require tremendous power, and for this reason the FM transmitting gear could not simply be added to the other communication functions of a multipurpose satellite. An entire satellite would have to be devoted to this single purpose of reaching the Soviet people. It would cost at least $25 million to build—a quarter of the Voice of America's annual budget for broadcasting to the entire world—and further millions to launch.

The satellite would be able to beam programs to Soviet listeners without the need for any modifications of their FM sets. More important, they would not have to install special antennas, an important point in a police state. Jamming would be difficult because the Soviet jammers would drown out the signals of their own stations.

The FM broadcasting satellite, in short, seems the perfect technical solution to reaching Soviet audiences, even if its price tag is a little high. The political considerations are another matter entirely. Relations between the United States and the Soviet Union would have to be at a far warmer state than they have been most of the years since World War II to permit such broadcasts. Launching the satellite at a time of poor relations would bring some kind of strong reaction—perhaps an intensive effort at outer-space jamming, crippling the transmitter, or downing the satellite. At a time of good relations, this expensive and elaborate means of reaching the Soviet people might be considered less of a priority, although it should be remembered that it is precisely during these rare periods that Soviet listeners do receive more reliable information about the West—both through the fairer treatment in their own media and the cessation of jamming.

The shooting down of Western satellites is most frequently mentioned in terms of those transmitting television signals into Soviet homes. Andrei Gromyko, the Soviet Foreign Minister, has said clearly that such satellites were enemies that should be shot down. His views were echoed by a member of the Politburo of a neighboring Communist country in a conversation with the author. "It would be simply too powerful a challenge to their position," he said. "They would feel out of control of their own population and opinion." His own more liberal government would not feel threatened by such a satellite, he added, since its media are more trusted by the people, and give them a more accurate picture of the world outside and shortcomings at home.

Such threats of space warfare have their diplomatic parallels at the United Nations, where the Soviet Union and its allies pressed for years for a ruling against satellite television broadcasts across international frontiers without the receiving nation's permission. They lined up 108 nations for the non-binding resolution that finally emerged. Thirteen, including the United States, Israel, and most Western European nations, were opposed. The key provision of the resolution says that a state planning direct television broadcasts from satellites "shall without delay notify the proposed receiving state or states of such intention and shall promptly enter into consultation with any of those states which so requests."

In practice, this would mean that a Voice of America television executive would have to contact the Soviet embassy in Washington to consult on whether there would be any objections to the prime-time screening of the Solzhenitsyn *Gulag* series. Such consultations would be likely to be short and heated. In fact, the Soviet Union could be expected to object to practically anything a Voice of America television service would plan to transmit; if it did not, the VOA people would worry about the quality of their programming.

The way thus seems pretty effectively barred for the deliberate DBS transmission of television programs designed, written, and produced by one government for broadcast to the subjects of another government.

Accidental reception is another matter. For years, American viewers have been poaching television programs from satellites with homemade dish antennas or kits bought from electronics stores. They get the same programs their neighbors have to pay for on cable, since they are intercepting a satellite signal intended for the large dish receiver of the cable company. Satellite piracy has international dimensions, too. Big dishes in Central America and the Caribbean catch the spillover from American satellites in position over United States viewing areas. The pirates include individuals who can watch Home Box Office without fee, hotels able to offer guests a wide range of entertainment, and even government and private broadcasting organizations, which then relay the signals to their audiences. There are an estimated 300,000 pirate dishes in the United States and thousands more around its borders.

The basic principle of DBS is: The stronger the signal, the smaller the dish antenna needed to pull it in. Conversely, weak signals require large dishes. Those who live in fringe areas sometimes have to mount fifteen- or twenty-foot affairs on trailers.

Television pirating in the Soviet Union has been limited to the reception of foreign signals broadcast from ground transmitters, not satellites, along the borders and seacoasts. It was possible to put up a dish and intercept the transmissions of Soviet domestic satellites, but, except for those in remote areas, there was no point to it—the programs would have been the same as those available from the local station. All this has changed, with the flurry of satellite transmission activity over Western Europe and Japan, to bring DBS into millions of homes.

The European Space Agency's map of the eight European television transmitters positioned at nineteen degrees west shows a series of interlocking loops, some circular and some oval, covering the western part of the continent. Some of the lines, however, range far to the east. The West German transmission footprint takes in all of East Germany, part of Poland, and the Czech or western half of Czechoslovakia. Italy's loop of territory includes the Yugoslav coast; both German and Italian footprints extend close to Hungary. To the East, Japan's Yuri satellite covers the entire coastal region of the Soviet Far East.

These spillovers are technically necessary if the footprint is to serve every part of the nation transmitting the signal, since national boundaries are a good deal more irregular than satellite beam patterns. Only the Japanese footprint makes its mark directly on Soviet soil, but the others come quite close. The eastern edge of Italy's circle is about 500 miles from the Ukraine; the West German footprint's furthest point east, in Poland, is only 250 miles from the Soviet border.

As the television pirates of Central America know, a signal can be picked up with ease six hundred miles from the edge of the footprint and with more effort much further away. Belize is eight hundred airline miles from the southernmost edge of American satellite footprints. It runs seven channels from pirated signals. Panama, fifteen hundred miles away, has a cable company with five thousand subscribers getting American transmissions.

But citizens of Panama and Belize can construct huge dishes to pull in "Dallas" and baseball games without worrying about the political police. A huge dish, or even a small one, on a Soviet rooftop would attract as much attention as a czarist flag.

Fortunately for Soviet viewers, the technological direction satellite transmitters and receivers are taking is toward more powerful signals and smaller dishes. The new European transmitters will be beaming programs that can be picked up on a dish two feet in diameter. Those benefiting most from this will be the viewers in Poland, Czechoslovakia, Yugoslavia, and East Germany, because they will have reception in the primary area of the footprint. Soviet piraters will have to use larger dishes.

Anyone reasonably handy can assemble such a dish, if not from flattened-out borscht pots then from aluminum, or even papier-mâché and foil. There is a small electronic device between dish and television set to convert the signal for home use; that, too, is no great task for a Soviet electronics hobbyist.

Vital to the whole enterprise is the fact that the dish can be installed *under* the roof, in an attic, shed, or loft, rather than on top. Satellite signals won't penetrate slate or tin roofs, but they will go through thin wood shingles. Some antenna spaces might have to be modified, with heavy beams trimmed or moved.

Some of the European signals are scrambled, to prevent pirating by those in the country of origin who do not want to pay. But others need no decoders. Soviet diplomats are understood to be urging Western European broadcasters to scramble everything, but this is a process that could cost companies millions of extra dollars with no return except for satisfied foreign censors.

The trend toward miniaturization will continue in every branch of DBS and television set design. With Japanese color television sets shrunk to the size of a billfold, black-and-white sets as small as wristwatches, and screens reduced to an inch and a half, it does not require flights of science fiction fantasy to visualize a television set that can be carried—and concealed—in a coat pocket, complete with a tiny dish that will connect its owner, whether Soviet or Panamanian, to the best television the world has to offer.

Muggeridge calls this the second revolution in international broadcasting, the first being the development of the transistor. It has too much power, politically and technologically, for the Soviet Union and other closed societies to hold it back, he thinks. Jamming is possible, he concedes; "nevertheless, we in the BBC are convinced that, though it may take many years to reach the world in general, the second revolution will come, though we envisage it developing side by side with the traditional use of shortwave, which we see as remaining important for some time."

The BBC's own television satellite for domestic DBS will be a part of this process. Its footprint covers a large area of the continent, with reception likely far to the east. As Muggeridge points out, areas too far out of range to pick up the picture signal may get the audio that accompanies it.

"The experts in the communications industry say that it may not be long before the special receiving equipment needed for DBS signals will be inexpensive enough for this form of broadcasting to reach mass audiences around the world," he said. "Then, further in the future, we may truly enter the era of space-age broadcasting, with stations that do not need special receiving equipment but can beam their signals directly into ordinary radio or television receivers."

"If anything like that happened, the Soviet regime wouldn't last a week," an émigré in New York said.

"So Russians learn that other people are better off. People in India already know this. What difference does it make to them?" another asked.

Pocket television sets are not going to overthrow the Soviet government. But neither is the communications revolution going to pass the Soviet Union by without effect. The microchips and glass fibers are pulling it closer to the rest of the world with a force it cannot resist if it wants to compete in that world.

The Soviet Union is likely to face up to the information revolution in the same way it has faced other challenges: by delaying, handing out a concession here and taking another away, retreating, regrouping, and hoping in the end that it can have both control over information and the benefits of open information exchange.

The result is likely to be more penetration of the Soviet Union by independent information, tolerated grudgingly by a regime that cannot stop all the leaks, and a concomitant improvement in the information available domestically.

The Communist-ruled countries of Eastern Europe have lived with this situation since their regimes were established after World War II. Editors and broadcasters in these countries readily admit that they have to permit more information to reach their publics because they know the publics will get it anyway from the West. Only one Soviet editor of the many I interviewed made this same concession. He puts out a paper in Tallinn, Estonia, where he can assume that his readers have a regular supply of uncensored news and commentary from across the Baltic on the Finnish television transmissions.

It will not be too long before every Soviet editor is in the position of the man in Tallinn and his counterparts in Eastern Europe. Information from the West will force them to be more candid. The process will be gradual, and in some places, barely perceptible; stronger forces than transistors and satellites have tried, and failed, to Westernize and liberalize Russia.

The Soviet Union is different in many ways from Eastern Europe (and its own Baltic republics). These societies have been used to a press that was at least intermittently free. They have always been much more exposed to Western culture, travel, and information than have Russia and the Soviet Union. These cultural differences go back to the Renaissance, which influenced much of Eastern Europe, but never reached Russia. They cannot be bridged in a year or two. But the new technology will quicken the process, bringing more of the world to the Soviet Union, if its leaders permit it, and, in some measure, even if they don't.

What will emerge is a better-informed Soviet public. It will not be a voting public in any meaningful sense, although it will know more about the power of elections in other countries. It will not be able to demand leadership changes through the weight of its opinion, although it may begin to express its opinions more frankly as it sees some of the rest of the world getting results by doing that. Such a public, more aware of events and issues inside and outside Soviet borders, will have great power, even if it is denied the formal institutions for wielding it for a time.

Its main contribution could be to force the next generation of leaders in the Kremlin to explain their policies and processes of decision-making a little more thoroughly and openly. That may not seem like much. But it could cause those leaders to consider their policies more carefully before they decide to imprison another scientist, writer, or peace activist, or invade another country. It could even cause them not to take those actions at all.

INDEX